PREACHING
about the
M A S S

PREACHING
about the
MASS

HOMILIES BY

GABE HUCK

BULLETIN INSERTS BY

ELIZABETH HOFFMAN

DAVID PHILIPPART

THERESA PINCICH

VICTORIA TUFANO

REFLECTION QUESTIONS BY

PETER MAZAR

LITURGY TRAINING PUBLICATIONS

ACKNOWLEDGMENTS

Copyright © 1992, Archdiocese of Chicago. All rights reserved. Liturgy Training Publications, 1800 North Hermitage Avenue, Chicago IL 60622-1101; 1 800 933-1800.

This book was designed by Jill Smith and typeset by Phyllis Martinez in Trump Mediæval and Lubalin Graph. Cover art by Barbara Searle. Photographs on pages 2, 12, 42, 72 and 82 are by Antonio Pérez. Photographs on pages 22, 32, 52, 62 and 92 are by Dorothy Perry. Sarah Huck assisted the editor, David Philippart. *Preaching about the Mass* was printed in the U.S.A.

03 02 01 00 99 98 97   7 6 5 4 3 2

MASS
ISBN 0-929650-47-6

CONTENTS

HOW TO USE—AND NOT TO USE—THIS BOOK

When the Second Vatican Council called for the "full, conscious, and active participation" of all the faithful in the liturgy, most parishes responded well. After more than a quarter of a century of renewal, our assemblies are comfortable with spoken parts—and to a lesser extent sung parts—of the Mass. Our gestures have evolved: for example, standing to receive bread (often in our hands now) *and* cup instead of kneeling to receive only the bread. And the restoration of distinct liturgical ministries has led to great numbers of people serving as acolytes, ushers, lectors, cantors, choristers, ministers of communion or members of the liturgy committee. This has resulted from and led to a lot of activity: workshops, training sessions and rehearsals in addition to the active celebrations themselves. So while we have much to refine in terms of how *well* we do things, we have made great progress in terms of active participation. But how conscious are our assemblies (parish leadership included) about what all this activity means?

The Council's goal was *full* participation, and that requires that the participation of all the faithful be not only active but also conscious. Conscious participation requires more (but not less) than knowledge about the Mass. It requires that we live deeply immersed in the liturgy and that we reflect on it.

This book is a tool to help parish leaders promote the conscious participation of the assembly in the Mass. There are several ways of using it, and there are a few ways it should not be used.

PREACHING AT MASS

A primary way of promoting the conscious participation of the assembly in the Mass is to *preach* it *at* Mass. But be careful! This book is not a collection of "canned" sermons to be scheduled in a sermon series ("Coming on the Sundays of August: Fr. Fred Explains the Mass!"). Instead, the chapters of this book are examples of what homilies on the Mass might sound like. They are offered to inspire the preacher and those who assist in homily preparation to go and seek the right words for their place and time.

But isn't the homily supposed to be on the readings? The *General Instruction of the Roman Missal* says:

> The homily is an integral part of the liturgy.... It is necessary for the nurturing of the Christian life. It should develop some point of the readings *or another text from the Ordinary or from the Proper of the Mass of the day*, and take into account the mystery being celebrated and the needs proper to the listeners. (#41, emphasis added)

Who celebrates the rites (the assembly), the rites themselves (texts and gestures) and the material objects used (the building itself, altar, ambo and font, for example) are all appropriate subjects for preaching at Mass if they are woven into a homily and not hammered into a lecture.

PREACHING (NOT TEACHING) THE MASS

Teaching about the Mass is a serious responsibility of parish leaders. The evolution of the Mass and of how the church understands it, the anthropological, sociological and psychological significance of ritual sacrifice and meal — these issues deserve attention. Catechesis on the Mass routinely should be available for all parishioners, from those of school age to those who are retired. Some resources for teaching about the

Mass are listed in the bibliography on page 102. But there is a difference between preaching and teaching, and this book is not about teaching.

The homily's purpose is not primarily to impart information. Before deciding to preach about the Mass at Mass, parish leaders would do well to review the purpose of a homily by reading *Fulfilled in Your Hearing: The Homily in the Sunday Assembly*. This document, from the Bishops' Committee on Priestly Life and Ministry, reminds us that "the homily is preached in order that a community of believers who have gathered to celebrate the liturgy may do so more deeply and more fully — more faithfully — and thus be formed for Christian witness in the world" (#43). It also says that the homily is not a lecture but a "scriptural interpretation of human existence which enables a community to recognize God's active presence in faith through liturgical word and gesture, and beyond the liturgical assembly, through a life lived in conformity with the gospel" (#81).

To enable the assembly to celebrate the liturgy more deeply, fully, faithfully — this is the purpose of preaching about the Mass. To do so requires that the homily be more poetry than prose, more an interpretation of meaning than an exposition of facts.

PREPARING TO PREACH ABOUT THE MASS

Thus preparing to preach about the Mass is crucial. The homilies in this book can aid preparation, never substitute for it.

The model for preparing a homily that is given in chapter 4 of *Fulfilled in Your Hearing* invites others to give the preacher input as the homily takes shape. Four or five people gather for an hour or so at the beginning of the week. They read the assigned scriptures aloud and each person then speaks the words or phrases that struck him or her. Someone who had previously agreed to do so then gives a brief (ten minutes) exegesis of the texts. The group then discusses (1) the good news it hears in these texts, (2) the challenge these texts offer the parish, and (3) what difference hearing these texts proclaimed in the liturgy might make in the parish. Finally the group prays in thanksgiving.

This model can be used to prepare for preaching about the Mass. If no homily preparation group exists, the parish staff or the liturgy committee might take this role. Depending on the Sundays chosen for preaching about the Mass (see below), the group may listen to the scriptures of the Sunday or to a selection of other texts from the liturgy and the relevant documents. It may be good for the group to read aloud the appropriate homily from this book. Lectionary and sacramentary should be at hand, along with copies of the reflection questions in this book.

The group might have some moments of silence before the example homily is read aloud. After the group has heard the homily, let each one simply state (no need for discussion at this point) what idea struck her or him most strongly. This might take about ten minutes. The preacher should listen carefully. Then, using the reflection questions that follow, the group can discuss for a half hour or so the parish's experience. This will give the preacher some insight into how to address the assembly. The preacher can take notes about how the parish experiences this particular part of the Mass and determine where new interpretations of meaning might be helpful.

As Sunday draws near, the preacher finalizes the text of the homily, incorporating input from the group and making the homily specific to the assembly that will hear it. Practicing the homily aloud before one or two listeners on Friday or Saturday would help ensure good delivery.

WHEN TO PREACH THE MASS AT MASS

There is one season in which it is always fitting to preach the Mass: Easter. As the rites of initiation of adults have reminded us, the fifty days of Easter are a time of *mystagogy*. Mystagogy literally means "recognizing the mystery." The Sundays of Easter flow from the Vigil in which the community experiences anew each year its mysteries: baptism, anointing, eucharist. It was once a common and wise practice for the preachers to spend the following Sundays preaching these basic deeds. There are various ways to preach the eucharist. The approach taken here is to begin with the rite itself — something the assembly *knows* and *does.* This is the approach of mystagogy.

xiii

While it is not a good idea to force a connection between a homily about the Mass and the assigned scriptures, the readings for the Sundays of Easter nonetheless offer stories, images and words with which to preach about the Mass. The story of the disciples gathered in fear and wonder behind locked doors, the encounter on the road to Emmaus ("Were not our hearts burning within us as he opened up the scriptures to us?"), the invitation to those fishing ("Come and eat your meal"), the description of the early church as being "devoted to the breaking of the bread and prayers" — these offer the poetic context in which to preach about the Mass.

It may not be necessary to even mention this in the homily, though. If great care is taken in proclaiming the scriptures, the powerful words, phrases and images will reverberate in the assembly and a homily about the Mass will follow appropriately even without explicit reference to the readings.

USING THIS BOOK FOR EASTERTIDE PREACHING

The first six homilies in this book are models for preaching from the Second Sunday of Easter to the Seventh. They "recognize the mystery" by reflecting on the assembly, its gathering, its listening to the word (two parts), its giving thanks and praise (two parts).

The last four homilies in this book approach the same mystery of the assembly's role at Mass from a different perspective. Instead of going through the rite from start to finish, these homilies address the elements of rite: song, posture, movement and the material objects we use. They may be used independently or in place of homilies three, four, five and six on the Sundays of Easter. Homilies one and two might precede them if they are used consecutively.

OTHER TIMES

Listening carefully to the liturgical year and the lectionary may suggest other times when preaching the Mass is appropriate. In Year B, for example, the 16th through 21st Sundays in Ordinary Time proclaim the bread of life passages from the Gospel of John. The imagery and poetry of these scriptures suggest preaching the Mass. Homilies one and ten are good models for preaching at the dedication of a church building, or its anniversary.

There are times other than Sunday when it would be beneficial to preach the Mass. These include a parish mission, various catechetical gatherings or an evening of recollection for liturgical ministers.

THE BULLETIN INSERTS

After each homily in this book (and before the reflection questions) are two bulletin inserts that the original purchaser of this book may reproduce for use in one parish. Either will serve as a reminder of the homily for people to mull over later.

The longer version is camera-ready, designed to be put on the copy machine and distributed as a handout after Mass. Or it may be patched directly into the parish bulletin. The shorter version is meant to be typed into a bulletin or newsletter when space is not available for the more complete form.

XV

THE APPLAUSE WAS SO LOUD

People will enjoy good preaching about the liturgy; we always have. Visiting Jerusalem in the fourth century, when Cyril was bishop, the pilgrim Egeria wrote home (to what was then Gaul) about the liturgies in the holy city. She describes how during each day of Easter week, the newly baptized and the rest of the faithful gathered to hear the bishop preach about the sacraments of initiation in the Church of the Holy Sepulcher: "The newly baptized come into the Anastasis, and any of the faithful who wish to hear the mysteries, but no catechumen comes in, and the doors are kept shut in case any try to enter. The bishop relates all that has been done [at the Easter Vigil] and interprets it, and, as he does so, the applause is so loud that it can be heard outside the church. Indeed the way he expounds the mysteries and interprets them cannot fail to move his hearers."

Perhaps preaching about the Mass in our parishes won't elicit such thunderous applause, but if done with care and with strength, it will move the church toward that full and conscious participation that is the right and duty of all the baptized.

xvi

HOMILY I

THE ASSEMBLY

When we meet here on Sunday, a lot of what we do is centered on a book, and a lot of what we do is centered on a table. What is this book? It is simply hundreds of pages on which are written the words of our scriptures, our Bible. The words of scripture are set down there according to the Sundays of the year. Much of our time together on Sunday, then, is spent in reading aloud those words and in reflecting on them in the psalm and homily.

And what is this table? Just as the book is made to be a beautiful and worthy way to carry the words of scripture, so the table is a beautiful and worthy way to hold bread and wine. Over this bread and wine, our community gives thanks and praise to God, then shares in holy communion the body and blood of Christ.

Gathering around the book and around the table — that is what we do together on Sunday. Because this is so central to our identity as Catholics, so important in our lifelong striving to be good Catholics, we need now and then to think on this Sunday liturgy and how we do it together.

Before the reader ever opens the book on Sunday morning, several things have to happen. The most basic thing is: There has to be an assembly. The liturgy is not done by a priest-presider with help from a musician and a lector. The liturgy on Sunday is done by an assembly — people gathered. Baptized Catholics come together. We do not come to be an audience, to be spectators while the specialists do their work. None of us is here to watch. That's hard for us to grasp. Most of our buildings are set up still as if there were the watchers and the watched, the audience and the performers. That is a carryover from a time of several centuries when "pay, pray and obey" was the way to be a Catholic.

The liturgy that is developing now from the reform begun at the Second Vatican Council is a liturgy that all of us baptized people do together, that we know how to do and love to do.

Somehow we are all both privileged and obliged to come here on Sunday—not to "go to" Mass, not to "attend" Mass, but together to celebrate the Mass, together to do the Mass. It is the privilege of the baptized: Only those who are baptized into the death of Christ and live now in Christ can make the prayer and communion at this altar. And it is our obligation: We baptized must do this on Sunday. The church has a rule about attending Mass on Sunday. The point of that rule is not to burden Catholics. The point is to make one thing very plain: Each baptized person of this parish is needed here on Sunday. What we do here takes all of us. We aren't obliged to come and watch, but to come and do.

During our time together each Sunday, the church is doing in this room what the church needs to do, hungers and thirsts to do, in order to be the church. The deeds are done not simply by one individual and another individual, but by the church here assembled. The body of Christ is proclaiming itself to be the body of Christ. The body of Christ—you and me—is identifying itself, remembering itself, preparing itself to live as Christ all week long. When we come into this room, we do not come to pray alone for an hour or so. We come to place ourselves beside brothers and sisters and to give all that wc have to give to the work the church has to do here. It is the church that listens to God's loving word, it is the church that then intercedes, it is the church that gives God thanks and praise over bread and wine, and it is the church that takes and is the holy communion. None of us does this alone, yet the church does nothing without each of us doing all we can.

But we come here as very human, very distracted, very preoccupied with our own worries, our own agendas, even our own prayers. How then can there be a church, a body of Christ? Maybe the question is: In a world with so many worries, agendas and prayers, how can there not be a church? How can we not be filled with an eagerness for this one time a week when we can gather all that worry and agenda and prayer and so much else up into the very body of Christ? It is hard, certainly. Everything around us says we are to live and strive and suffer and grow alone. We are so private, so on our own. So it is difficult to come here and be told—yes, you as an individual person are God's beloved, as is every brother and sister of ours of every race and religion and condition in all the world. Yes. But here, here we are to set all that aloneness aside, because this is the church. God called us in Christ into a church, a body, and it is that body God speaks to; it is that body that prays here today; it is that body that sings and gives thanks and is nourished in holy communion. We are that body! Baptism made us so. God's word each Sunday makes us so. The eucharist we do here and the communion we share here make us so.

Each Sunday we follow many paths to these doors. We come through these doors into the house of the church. Our house. We come into this meeting place—a meeting place for each other, a meeting place for the church and its saints and its Lord. In some parishes, the doors of the building bring the assembling people right up against the baptism place. Sunday after Sunday, the font and its water recall that this is indeed the entrance to the church—baptism into Christ's death, baptism to life in Christ's body, the church. In places where the font is so approachable, the people assembling each Sunday can take its water and sign themselves with the cross. But in all of our churches, water is placed by the door. All of us take this water on our hand and with it sign ourselves with the cross. Here, we say, "I acknowledge that in this room I am conscious of what I am a part of and who we are always: the body of Christ. In this room I let water remind me of my baptism into the church. In this room I let the sign of the cross remind me of the one to whom I belong. And so do I prepare for this deed, this Mass, we do together."

The bulletin insert on the next two pages can be reproduced, added to the parish bulletin or handed out after Mass. The shorter version that follows it can be typed into the bulletin if space is limited.

HOMILY I

6

WE GATHER TOGETHER

Day by day, people come together at different times in different places and groups for different purposes. And many of those times, we do nothing but be there — at most, we are a group of individuals together. Assembling at the bus stop or the train station, assembling in the school auditorium, assembling at the theater or the sports stadium — being there is all that is required. That is the purpose for this kind of assembling. But there are other times — at work, at a party, at a meal — when we assemble and we must do more that just be there. We must talk to each other, reach out our hand to each other, perhaps even sing with each other. We must participate in the action, the purpose of the assembly. If we do not, then our gathering is not an assembly, and we become merely a group of people who happen to be in the same place at the same time.

Are we an assembly when we come together on Sunday for the liturgy? Is just being there enough? Is being there and listening enough? Is being there and doing our own private praying enough? Don't we call ourselves the one body of Christ?

Remember the scriptural analogy of the body of Christ and the human body: "There are, indeed, many different members, but one body.... If one member suffers, all the members suffer with it; if one member is honored, all the members share its joy" (1 Corinthians 12:20, 26). Where in this world that stresses individualism can we make this vision of an assembled humanity a reality, if not when we come together at Sunday Mass?

For it is at Sunday Mass that we *assemble* to praise and to thank God — together. We ask for God's blessing and we pray for all people — together. We listen to the word and we sing — together. We receive the body and blood of Christ — together.

We know that as individual members of the body we are different and look different; we know that we don't always agree; we know that often we don't like one another. And that's okay. But at this liturgy we are called to go beyond all that makes us different, all that separates us one from another, to find and to express that which makes us one, that which makes us the body of Christ.

That's not easy — it's hard, even for one hour on Sunday. But it's what we, as baptized Catholics, are supposed to do. And if we can manage to be together as the body of Christ for one hour each week, maybe, just maybe, we can do it for a day, or a week, or ...

Preaching about the Mass, © 1992 Archdiocese of Chicago, Liturgy Training Publications, 1800 North Hermitage Avenue, Chicago IL 60622-1101; 1-800-933-1800. Text by Theresa Pincich. Design by Jill Smith.

WE GATHER TOGETHER

Day to day, people gather at different times in different groups and places for different purposes. Some of these times, we have nothing to do but be there — at most, we are a group of individuals together. Assembling at the bus stop or the train station, in the school auditorium, at the theater or the sports stadium — just being there is enough. At other assemblies — the work place, a party, a meal — we must do more than just be there. We must talk to each other, reach out our hand to each other, perhaps sing with each other. We must participate in the action to fulfill the purpose of the assembly; or it is not an assembly, merely a group of people who happen to be in the same place at the same time.

HOMILY I

9

What kind of an assembly are we when we gather on Sunday for liturgy? Is just being there enough?

What does being the body of Christ mean? Where in this world that stresses individualism can we make that a reality, if not when we come together at Sunday Mass? We *assemble* to praise and to thank God — together. We ask for God's blessing and we pray for all people — together. We listen to the word and we sing — together. It's not easy, but it's what we as baptized Catholics are supposed to do.

Preaching about the Mass, © 1992 Archdiocese of Chicago, Liturgy Training Publications, 1800 North Hermitage Avenue, Chicago IL 60622-1101; 1-800-933-1800. Text by Theresa Pincich. Design by Jill Smith.

REFLECTION QUESTIONS

1. "Each baptized person of the parish is needed here on Sunday." Why are you needed at Mass each week — what is your role? If you are missing, who notices? The words "company" and "companion" mean "those we break bread with." If you miss the Sunday eucharist, who will be deprived of your company?

2. Some folks say that they don't need to join with others to worship God; they can worship just fine alone. What are some differences between private prayer and public worship? Why is it necessary to worship with others?

3. We are a "sacramental church." That means we use sacraments — "holy signs" — when we worship. One of these holy signs is the coming together of people. The homily comments that we can be distracted at Mass even by our own prayers. What do you think it means to put aside private prayers, to come together with other people to take up the church's prayer? How can the Mass help people leave behind their "aloneness"?

4. How welcoming is the outside of the church building? What are a few ways that the church's parking lots, the landscaping and the entrances can be made more "user friendly"? How can ushers help offer hospitality? What are some ways that households and individuals can be more welcoming of each other at worship?

5. Imagine that you are the person seated farthest from the altar in the church. Can you see any of the faces of fellow parishioners? Does the seating arrangement make your church building feel more like a place to watch what happens or like a place to participate in communal activity? What long-term plans might make the layout better suited to worship?

HOMILY II

THE GATHERING RITE

What happens on Sunday when we have come through the door to this room, this house of the church, and have taken the water that identifies us as persons baptized into Christ, into the church?

Maybe to answer the question, What do we do?, ask: What is this gathering called? It is sometimes called "the congregation." What do we do? We congregate. It is sometimes called "the assembly." What do we do? We assemble. The first thing we have to do is congregate, assemble. Both those words mean "to get ourselves together." Like a lot of preliminaries, it isn't the most important thing that is going to happen. Except in this sense: If it doesn't happen, if we don't get ourselves together, then all the other things can't happen. It is like a good recipe. Turning on the oven isn't all that important, but if I don't turn it on, then no matter how carefully I mix the flour and baking soda and oil and milk, there isn't going to be any cake. That's how it is here. I can have a fine homily prepared, the song leaders can be rehearsed and ready, the acolytes and lectors and communion ministers know their service well, but if nobody turns on the oven, we can't get anywhere. And the oven is the assembling—our gathering together.

If I board a bus alone, I probably look for a seat alone. If I board a bus with a friend, we probably sit together, but we don't need to pay much attention to anyone else on the bus. That's a bus. We ask nothing more from a bus than that it take us from one spot to another. But if we come in here and act like we are on a bus—looking for a place to sit alone or just with a friend or family—we've misjudged what sort of thing is going on here. This isn't a bus, it is a boat that is rowed by everyone on board. It only goes when all the people move together. That's what liturgy is: something done by everyone together. Sure, different members have different roles, but the deed itself — moving the boat — is done by everyone.

That's a long way of saying that when we come through those doors, it's clear what we have to do. We have to make the church look like the church, act like the church, sound like the church. We have to congregate to make a congregation. We have to assemble to make an assembly. There are lots of times in life to come in here and pray alone. There are lots of times in life to pray alone wherever you are. But Sunday Mass is not one of those times. Sunday Mass is what we do together. That isn't a theory that will work no matter how we look in here, how we sound, how we act. It isn't a theory, it's practice. The church has to get itself together. If we work at it, all of us, maybe we'll come to a time when we'll walk through the door and, without even thinking about it, head for the empty place closest to the altar. If we work at it, we won't have to imagine that we are one in Christ; we'll act like we are. The room will fill from these seats to those seats to those and only as far out as there are people here. The reason, let's be clear on this, is not that there is some special holiness in getting close to the altar; the reason is that there is the holiness of the church in getting close to one another and doing this deed together. So, maybe we can begin. Come forward when we arrive. And if a row is empty, don't sit on the end protecting it — let us take a place in the middle of that row as if inviting others to sit beside us.

There should be graciousness in our gathering. Kindness and hospitality are not the enemies of peaceful assembling. Smiling, nodding in welcome even to those I do not know by name, greeting others warmly: These are building up the body of Christ. Ushers and sometimes other persons have the task of helping us in these first moments together: a greeting, help with getting to a seat, other hospitable deeds.

But ushers only specialize in what we must all do for one another: Make it clear that all alike are welcome here. That is why we have to do the best we can to make this place welcoming to all of us, those of us with disabilities, those with young children, those who are elderly.

Is all of this important because we are like a club or a group of intimate friends getting together? We are not like that at all. Almost the opposite. Here we welcome people who would probably never be our friends. What we have in common is far more than blood, far more than the mutual affection of friends. What we have in common is baptism in Christ. That's it. That's all that matters here. That's why rich and poor should be sitting side by side. Every barrier society erects to keep us apart is worthless here. Every bond society builds up to put us into this little group or that clan or the other club is also worthless here. In a sense, we are naked here, like a baby in the waters of baptism. All the externals are gone. All that we wear is Christ. We all wear Christ. And that — not simply that we might like one another — is why we come forward and ring this altar round.

That is the preparation for Mass. Such preparation goes a step further when we begin the gathering rites or entrance rites. Please don't think that "entrance rites" means the entrance of the priest who presides at the liturgy and the other ministers. It means the entrance of all of us together into the liturgy. Some may be in the ritual procession, but in reality we are all in procession, all moving into our liturgy. All the words and song and gesture are ways to get from where we are to where we want to be: a church ready to hear God's word. We get there with song and procession and the sign of the cross and prayer, and sometimes with sprinkled water or penitential prayers and the Gloria. At their best, these are things we all know how to do and do them fully and with a sense that here, in making the sign of the cross, in singing out loudly, in saying familiar words, here we are really at home, in our element, one with brothers and sisters making up the church.

There are at least three moments in these gathering rites when we have to do our work well. First, we sing. The song at the beginning of the liturgy is for all of us. It lets us know we are not in this room alone. We hear this news: A whole assembly is processing into this liturgy together. We sing to hear each other, to let our voice — good or poor as it is — get lost with all the other voices. We sing to signal the transition into communal activity.

Second, we make the sign of the cross. This simple gesture stands at the beginning of the liturgy because it stands at the beginning of the Christian life. The baby and the catechumen are claimed for Christ with this sign. It proclaims who we are and whose we are. We make it deliberately, with care. Remember, the liturgy is not what the priest who presides is doing: The liturgy is what the people are doing. The liturgy is this sign of the cross.

Third, just before the first reading, we pray. Sometimes we talk as if the whole liturgy is a prayer, but really there are all kinds of things that happen in the liturgy, and prayer is one of them. So we come to the moment when the presider first says, "Let us pray." Then we should be quiet together, be still and calm and aware of all these people silent and praying together. In the silence, simply prepare to pray. Then attend to the words of the prayer that is spoken by the presider and, if you can agree that this is indeed our common prayer, join in saying Amen.

HOMILY II

16

The bulletin insert on the next two pages can be reproduced, added to the parish bulletin or handed out after Mass. The shorter version that follows it can be typed into the bulletin if space is limited.

No one ever said it had to be perfect! Lucky for us. If we waited until we were able to come to Mass perfectly calm, perfectly prepared, or perfectly at peace, then some of us would probably never get there.

The reality for many of us is that we spend the hour or hours before arriving at church looking for a lost shoe, changing the baby's diaper, ironing the only clean blouse, trying to remember if we took our medication, arguing with offspring about why they have to go to Mass, struggling behind a motorist who insists on driving ten miles below the speed limit, trying to find the last parking space in the lot. And these experiences, some will tell us, are part of our gathering rite for Sunday Mass.

Yes, most of these "problems" could be avoided with careful planning — maybe preparing for Mass *should* begin the evening before.

Take that thought a little further. The time at Mass is spent with and for people we call our brothers and sisters. Perhaps then we *should* begin to prepare for this time a little earlier in the week, especially if we have some reconciling to do. At Mass we pray for the church and for the world. Maybe we *should* prepare still earlier in the week by listening to or reading about what is going on in our church and the world so that we know what to pray for or about. At Mass we listen to the word. *Should* we begin preparation even a little earlier in the week by reading the scriptures so they will be more familiar to us on Sunday?

Get the idea? We *should* always be working on what *should* be happening. But if we keep looking and waiting for what *should* be, we will miss what is real.

We come to the liturgy prepared as best we can — accepting that our preparation will be imperfect. This is not an excuse, but reality. We greet one another — we begin to

leave a little of the recent past behind. We sing together —
we hear other voices, perfect and imperfect. We make the
sign of the cross — a visible sign that we are the body of
Christ. And we pray — we make the transition from the
world of *should be* to the world of what is real: Christ present in the gathered church.

Preaching about the Mass, © 1992 Archdiocese of Chicago, Liturgy Training Publications, 1800 North Hermitage Avenue, Chicago IL 60622-1101; 1-800-933-1800. Text by Theresa Pincich. Design by Jill Smith.

IN THE GATHERED CHURCH

If we waited until we were able to come to Mass perfectly prepared, some of us would never get there.

The reality for many of us is that we spend the time before arriving at church looking for a lost shoe, ironing the only clean blouse, arguing with offspring about why they have to go to Mass, or crawling behind a motorist driving ten miles below the speed limit.

Things are never the way they *should* be. But if we keep waiting for what *should* be, we will miss what is real.

HOMILY II

19

We come to Mass prepared as best we can — accepting our imperfection. This is not an excuse but a fact. We greet one another — we leave behind a little of what distracts us. We sing together — we hear other voices, perfect and imperfect. And we pray — we make the transition from the world of *should be* to the world of what is real: Christ present in the gathered church.

Preaching about the Mass, © 1992 Archdiocese of Chicago, Liturgy Training Publications, 1800 North Hermitage Avenue, Chicago IL 60622-1101; 1-800-933-1800. Text by Theresa Pincich. Design by Jill Smith.

REFLECTION QUESTIONS

1. With whom do you usually sit at Mass? The homily suggests that there are a number of basic courtesies when choosing where to sit at Mass. What are some of these?

2. "If we don't get ourselves together, then all the other things can't happen." We're all learning, more and more, that at Mass if any part is done poorly, everything suffers. One of the first things to happen at Mass is our coming together. This either happens well or happens poorly. What is lost from the eucharist if we fail to welcome one another? If we fail to sit close to one another and to make it plain that it matters that we're worshiping together as a body?

3. "Here we welcome people who may never be our friends." Why is it important to worship alongside people who are different from us or who may not be our friends? What bond does baptism create among people that is closer than friendship or even than marriage?

4. Parish organizations tend to focus on various groups of people: senior citizens, students in religious education programs, parochial school students, teenagers, men, women, ethnic groups, single people or married people. In what ways can the parish help bring people together instead of separating them?

5. The liturgy should be a sign of unity in a parish. Why is it inappropriate to gear the liturgy to a particular group? Or, to ask the same question positively, why is it important that the liturgy involve all parishioners?

6. "We sing to hear each other." What are some ways to help our voices "get lost with all the other voices"? Does the seating arrangement in your church building make for better singing? How does singing together, or making a gesture together, or saying Amen to a common prayer help make us one people instead of a roomful of individuals?

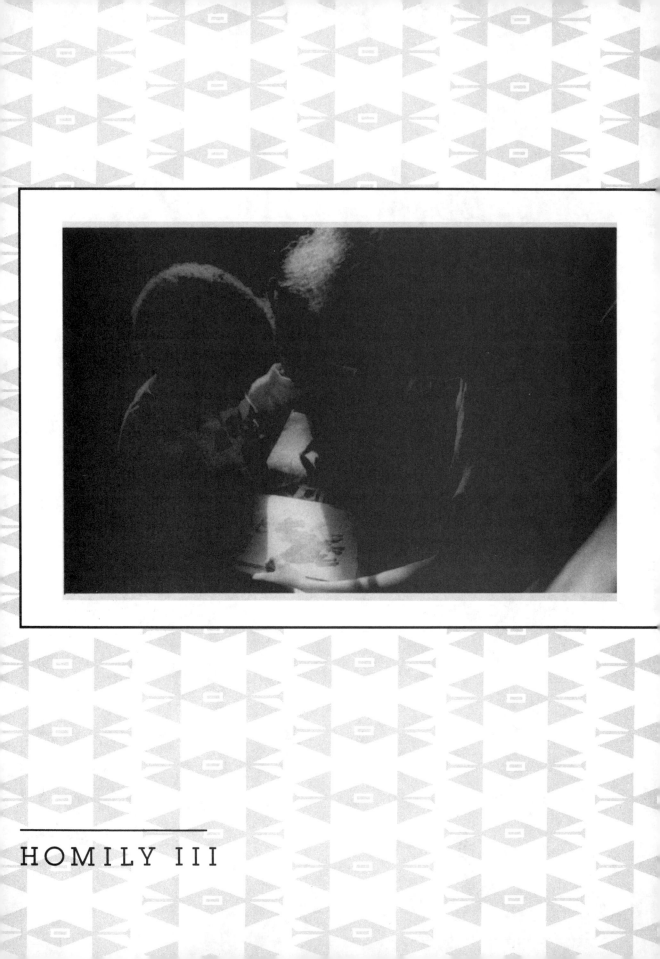

HOMILY III

THE LITURGY OF THE WORD I

What did we just do? We said, "Praise to you, Lord Jesus Christ," and sat down. Why were we standing? Why sitting now? Why the words, "Praise to you, Lord Jesus Christ"? And what is supposed to happen now? What should happen? What have we come to expect will happen when we are all sitting and one person is standing here to speak?

We talked earlier about how we come into this room, how the church gathers in its house. We talked about how the song and the sign of the cross and the prayer are ways of putting on the baptismal garment, being a congregation, an assembly, that is here to do its liturgy. By the time we finish those actions and sit down to listen to the reader, we should have a strong sense that what happens here is done by this church. We should also have a sense that this Sunday gathering is happening on a Sunday in Eastertime or in Lent or in Advent or just in the ordinary Sundays of the year. The song and the look of the room and the whole atmosphere tell us that.

So we come to the moment when the assembly sits and the reader stands with the book open. It happens each Sunday, but it should still be, every time, a moment of delight for us. Wherever we come from that morning, whatever the troubles, whatever the aches and pains, whatever the worries, whatever the delights, whatever the preoccupations, somehow they all get caught up into the troubles, aches and pains, delights and preoccupations that are sitting beside and behind and around each one of us. This is a church filled with such things. And it is a church about to listen to its book. What kind of a church is going to listen well to its book? One with no worries? Or one full of the struggles of everyday life? The truth is this: We come here as hungry individuals, needy people, and when we are all together, we are a hungry church.

The words of this book are our food and our drink. We sit down, and the reader opens the book, and the church is nourished. We know perhaps that the church asks that we not eat for an hour before Mass and communion. That is, indeed, just a symbolic fasting. But it is symbolic of this: that we are to come here hungry for God's word and hungry for the eucharist and holy communion. Each one of us must decide how we observe that fasting before Mass. In some way, it means that the Sunday liturgy does not begin with the first singing here, or even with entering through those doors. The Sunday liturgy began when each one of us woke up this morning and in the time from then to now when — by fasting or by other ways — we let our bodies and spirits and minds be hungry for God's word, hungry to praise and give thanks and share holy communion.

On most Sundays, we read three scriptures. The first is usually from the oldest books of the Bible, the Hebrew Scriptures. The second is always from the letters of the New Testament. The third is from the gospels: Matthew, Mark, Luke and John. We might think of it this way: As a people, we Catholics travel through the centuries, one generation to another. We carry with us a book. It is a book that we believe is the foundation of our life together as a people. In each generation it is read again and again and again, read in all the different places and times where this Catholic people finds itself. We see that we are not the only people with such a book. Other Christian churches journey with much the same book; Jews carry a book that contains most of these same contents — and they have carried it far longer. Most of our Christian book is, in fact, a Jewish book and we would do well to understand that.

Now this book that the Catholic people carry has within it a great many smaller books. And they contain all sorts of writing: legends, myths, histories, genealogies, laws,

HOMILY III

24

customs, wise sayings, humor, poetry, songs of every kind from love songs to war chants, prophecy, letters, sermons, parables, biography. Through the course of three years, the book is opened on Sundays to many parts of this collection. Sometimes, for week after week, we read in order from one book. We do this especially with the second readings. This [summer, fall], for example, we will be reading through Paul's letter to the church at [Rome, Corinth, etc.].

In the gospel readings, through much of each year, we go in order through Matthew, Mark or Luke. This order is broken when we come to the seasons of Advent, Lent and Eastertime; on some of those Sundays we do our reading from the gospel of John. Every three years, then, the Sunday readings give us most of the New Testament.

The first readings, except during Eastertime, come from the Hebrew Scriptures: from Genesis, Exodus, Deuteronomy, Kings, Wisdom, Isaiah, Jeremiah and many other books. These first readings often give us a word or an image that will be reflected in the gospel reading. More than anything, these first readings should encourage us to read widely in the Hebrew Scriptures, the books we have usually called the Old Testament.

So we are this Catholic people, and we carry with us a book that our parents and ancestors gave us and which we will give to our children. We read from it alone. We read from it in our households with family and friends. But always we read from it in our assembly. And that reading is not simply for our information. Nor is it just some formality. The reading is what gives this church its nourishment, even its identity, its life. And that is the hard part. We are used to going it alone; even with the Bible itself, we often try to think out what it means to *me*. But here the word is for the church. I listen because I am part of the church. I listen because if I don't, the church is that much less.

So when the book is opened — each time it is opened on a Sunday at liturgy — we fix our eyes on the reader and we listen. We are supposed to cling to the words, cling to them like life itself, for that is what they are. Any book or booklet that has the readings in it can be read to prepare or to follow through, but when the reading of God's word is taking place in front of us, then it is the spoken words of the reader we want to hear, not printed words on a page. It is common sense and simple respect that tells us to look at the one reading and hang on to every word.

Readers, for their part, are asked to spend a great deal of time with the scripture text to be read. They pour over it again and again. They practice it aloud. They are charged to make every effort in helping the church to hear this scripture. That means that they live with and wrestle with it all week long so that on Sunday they can let our scriptures come to us from one convinced of their worth and truth.

That part is hard. The part of the assembly, of all of us, is even harder. Talk is cheap, we say. We live in a sea of words, and most of them flow right by us. Here we are to have the habit of good, hard listening. Listen to hear a word you have not let into your mind and heart before. Listen for an image to guide us baptized people. Listen as you would to the voice and words of one who loves you. Don't try to think of how this word fits your life right now; don't try to find some hidden message. Just listen. Just be the church, here, today, on its journey, carrying its book, hungry for the words that are life to this people.

The bulletin insert on the next two pages can be reproduced, added to the parish bulletin or handed out after Mass. The shorter version that follows it can be typed into the bulletin if space is limited.

**WE HEAR
OUR STORY**

When Alex Haley, the author of the book *Roots*, decided to research his family's heritage, he began with the stories his mother and grandmother had told him as a child. They had passed on to him the memories that once had been handed on to them, the only record of who his people were, where they had come from, what they had suffered and what they had overcome. Armed with only these stories, not a complete history, but enough to begin with, Haley began to unravel his family's past. The thread that Haley was able to follow back through his ancestry led to the one the family's stories had called "the African." This young man, the tradition said, had gone out from his village one day to collect wood and was kidnapped by slave traders.

Through research in the records of slave ships, Haley was able to determine when and from what part of Africa his ancestor may have been taken. Traveling there, Haley met with the descendants of the people who had lived in the village that he believed his ancestor had come from. He was invited to sit with the community as the storyteller told their history. The story covered many centuries, and the storyteller chanted it from memory, as he had been taught.

At one point, the storyteller told of a young man, Kunta Kinte, who had gone out from the village one day to collect wood and who never returned. Haley told those gathered what had happened to the young man, and that he, Haley, was that man's descendant. The community gathered around Haley and welcomed him as one who had finally come home.

Every Sunday our Catholic community gathers to hear our story. The book from which that story is read is carried with reverence and with respect. We prepare to hear our story with singing and silence and prayer. We take the time to get ready, to put aside the cares that separate us from one another, to empty ourselves of noise and data so that we can hear the story; that makes of this gathering of individuals a people fashioned and chosen by God.

Over the course of three years, we will hear most of the New Testament and a large portion of the Old Testament. Our Christian story begins with the Jewish people. Their tradition and ours is told in legends, myths, histories, genealogies, laws, customs, wise sayings, prophecy, parables, letters and songs. Whatever form they take, these scriptures tell the story of a God who made and loved a people, a God who chose a people who could reveal to all who God is. But it is not enough to hear these words; we must recognize that these stories are ours, that the people in them are our people, that the God who called and loved them calls and loves us and is fashioning us into a people who can reveal to all who this God is. Then we will understand that when we gather with the community in faith we have come home.

Preaching about the Mass, © 1992 Archdiocese of Chicago, Liturgy Training Publications, 1800 North Hermitage Avenue, Chicago IL 60622-1101; 1-800-933-1800. Text by Victoria M. Tufano. Design by Jill Smith.

WE HEAR OUR STORY

Alex Haley, the author of the book *Roots*, began his research of his family's heritage by recalling the stories his mother and grandmother had told him as a child. Through research Haley was able to determine when and from what part of Africa his ancestor had been taken. Traveling there, Haley was invited to listen to the tribal history. At one point, the storyteller told of Kunta Kinte, who had gone out from the village one day and never returned. From the stories he had heard as a child, Haley recognized this as the story of how his ancestor had been captured into slavery. The community received Haley as one who had finally come home.

Every Sunday our Catholic community gathers to hear our story. Our story begins with the Jewish people. Their tradition and ours is told in legends, myths, histories, genealogies, laws, customs, wise sayings, prophecy, parables, letters and songs. Whatever form they take, these scriptures tell the story of a God who made and loved a people, a God who chose a people who could reveal to all who God is.

But it is not enough to hear these words; we must recognize that these stories are ours, that the people in them are our people, that the God who called and loved them calls and loves us and is fashioning us into a people who can reveal to all who this God is. Then we will understand that when we gather with the community in faith we have come home.

Preaching about the Mass, © 1992 Archdiocese of Chicago, Liturgy Training Publications, 1800 North Hermitage Avenue, Chicago IL 60622-1101; 1-800-933-1800. Text by Victoria M. Tufano. Design by Jill Smith.

REFLECTION QUESTIONS

1. The homily asks an important question: "What have we come to expect will happen when you are all sitting and one person is standing here to speak?" Often we get what we expect. What are your expectations of the readers? Of the homilist?

2. "Most of our Christian book is, in fact, a Jewish book, and we would do well to understand that." How does your parish help and encourage members to understand the Bible and, in particular, the Jewishness of this book?

3. The lectionary, the book of Bible passages read at Mass, is arranged according to a few simple principles. The author of the homily mentions several. For example, the second reading at Mass is usually from one of Paul's letters, read in order Sunday by Sunday. Flip through a lectionary and see how this happens. What letters of Paul will be read this year? Is anything in the works to help people study these letters?

4. On Sundays through much of a year we read in order through a particular gospel. In 1992 we read mostly from Luke; in 1993, from Matthew; in 1994, from Mark. What is the parish doing to help people become better acquainted with this year's gospel? How can the homilist help?

5. Our tradition is to listen attentively — and not to read along — while the readers proclaim the scriptures at Mass. Is that what usually happens here on Sundays? Can you hear and understand the readers? Does the arrangement of the church or the lectern or the sound system need adjustment to help people see and hear the readers better?

6. "Here we are to have the habit of good hard listening." Readers need to hone certain skills to make them better readers. What skills do listeners need to develop?

HOMILY IV

THE LITURGY OF THE WORD II

The gospels tell us stories about how Jesus and the disciples would take part in the gatherings in the synagogue on the Sabbath. At the time of Jesus it had already long been the practice of Jews to come together on that day for public reading and reflection on the scriptures. This is how Jesus grew up. He was among a people who gave the texts of the Law and the Prophets honor and attention in their lives.

Those who later came to believe in Jesus through the preaching of the disciples continued this practice. They, too, read from the Law and the Prophets and added some part of a letter from Paul, perhaps, and later some of the texts that were going to make up the gospels. We continue in the same way today. So do all the synagogues and churches in the world. On the Sabbath, Jews now, as then, read from the Law and the Prophets, and this is the text for the preaching. On Sunday, Christians gather and read from these Hebrew Scriptures and also from their Christian Scriptures, and these are usually the texts for the preaching. Jews and Christians are peoples of the book. The book, opened and read each seven days for the whole community, is handed on from one generation to the next, and in each generation it is heard fresh and alive. Among Christians, some have the custom of leaving the selection of a scripture text to the preacher. Catholics and many other churches, like most Jewish congregations, have a cycle of readings from the scripture. We call this our lectionary: It is an order of readings for three years of Sundays. That is the book that we carry here with great honor in our procession each Sunday, that we open and read from and listen to and preach about.

Much surrounds this reading. At the beginning, we sit down and listen as a lector reads to us. The task is to give full attention to the words of the reader. What happens when this first reading is concluded? The reader announces its conclusion by saying: The word of the Lord. And we respond with an ancient phrase that was *"Deo gratias"* in Latin and is "Thanks be to God" in English. It is a line like "Good morning" or "God bless you," an almost automatic expression, but one that reveals an attitude of thanksgiving.

And then we need some silence. Why? It helps perhaps to know an image the church uses for the liturgy of the word. It calls it a foundation. Foundation. Support. The basics. That which holds up everything else. That without which everything else is going to fall. Now, the church calls the liturgy of the word the foundation not just of the liturgy, but of our life. So what we are doing here is laying a foundation. Week after week, we keep at it. If we fail here, we can't hope for much anywhere else. So we take our time. That's the reason for the silence. We are not hasty about the liturgy of the word.

That's hard. We are people who think that silence means something is wrong. But silence here is right. Silence means we have time for this. We don't have to rush. We can let the foundation take shape and settle. We can sit back in this tiny silent time and let a single word or phrase from the reading sound again and again inside us.

That silence grows into a psalm. Whenever possible, this psalm is sung, usually with all of us alternating with a cantor or the choir. What are psalms, and why are we singing one every Sunday after the first reading? The psalms are in the Bible in a book by that name. There are 150 of them there. They had all been composed by the time of Jesus, and the scriptures show us that Jesus and his friends knew these songs well and used them in their prayer. Some psalms are songs of blessing; some, of cursing. Some are ballads telling stories; some are harsh lamentations. Some are pure praise of God; some cynical challenges to God's apparent indifference to human suffering. There are psalms like "The Lord is my shepherd" that are as well known to many Christians as the Lord's Prayer, and there are psalms we know because Jesus prayed them: "My God, my God, why have you forsaken me" was a psalm that he repeated on the cross. The psalms were basic texts of Jewish liturgy in Jesus' day — that is how he learned them — and they remain so today. Among Christians, they became the core of daily prayer for hermits, nuns and monks, but for centuries many psalms were also the basic daily prayer of ordinary baptized people. In the initial reforms of the liturgy after Vatican II, a step was taken to give the psalms back to all of us. Usually our part is only one line, a short refrain. This we should be able to learn by heart so that we can sit and sing without book or song sheet. That refrain we sing is usually one line from the psalm itself. Brief as it is, it might become a tiny prayer for us during the day and week. In that way, the psalms do their ancient work: They teach us to pray. They show us how many ways we need for speaking to God. The psalm is not an easy moment in the liturgy. It seldom brings us to our feet. It takes some work, some attention. It asks that we be in for the long haul.

HOMILY IV

35

It's another story for the song that comes moments later. After the second reading and its silence are done, the whole assembly stands up and begins to sing alleluias. It is our procession into the gospel reading. The Alleluia is not the only mark of special attention given the gospel. Candles and sometimes incense accompany the person who is to read the gospel, so that the reading may be surrounded with light and with fragrance. Every sense is involved. Before the gospel is read, the text is announced, and we respond, "Glory to you, Lord," and as we do so, we sign our forehead, lips and heart with the cross. With this gesture we show that the gospel speaks to our minds, forms our words, changes our hearts. After the gospel, the reader proclaims: "This is the gospel of the Lord," and we say, "Praise to you, Lord Jesus Christ." Then the reader kisses the words on the page. We saw the kiss at the beginning of the liturgy when the presider approached the holy table and kissed it. We will see it again — though often in the form of a handshake — at the peace greeting. Here this gesture of love is made for the words of the holy gospel.

All of this — Alleluia, the standing posture we take, procession, candles, announcement of the text, tiny signs of the cross, closing acclamation, kiss — all show the place the gospel holds in this community, this church. We surround the gospel with such signs of reverence and affection because that gospel is for us the saving power of God.

The homily comes then, usually as the effort of one person who has pondered the readings to see what they might mean in the life of this church. That pondering is both lonely and social. The homilist has to do this work alone, to wrestle with these scriptures, but also has to be thoroughly familiar with the life this church lives and in the life of the whole world. Gospel and world bang together in the homily.

The homilist is not the only one charged to confront the scriptures. We all have to do that. If we only meet the scriptures for a few moments each week in this place, we have little sense for how to listen, little sense for the scriptures' power and breadth. The public reading of scripture here is meant for people who have some presence to the scriptures all week long. The Bible — family edition or pocket edition — is no stranger to Catholics. If only one thing can be done in a busy life, then let it be a quiet reading at home of these texts during the week.

Silent time for reflection follows the homily, then we stand and recite one of the ancient formulas of faith, a creed, a way of summing up the belief of this church. Before we can do this, on most Sundays those who are preparing for baptism are dismissed. What is to follow — the creed, intercessions, eucharist — is for the baptized alone. This is not easy to do, to send people out of this assembly, but it is a measure of how seriously we take our baptism. It is only baptism that allows us to profess faith, ask of God what we need and give thanks and praise through Christ.

The liturgy of the word concludes with prayers of intercession, called the prayer of the faithful. Sometimes it is sung, sometimes spoken. It is a litany, the kind of prayer where our part stays the same and the leader brings, one after another, many things before us. After hearing and taking to heart the word of God, the church does something here that gets to the work of being a Christian. We intercede. We pray to God for all that this world and this church longs for. We are telling God to remember: the oppressed, the suffering, the sick, the addicted, the victims of war and famine, the imprisoned, the dying, the leaders, the many, many, many troubles and needs of the whole world. Whatever else the church may be, it is an assembly that will not let God forget. It is an assembly that keeps its eyes open, because we have by our baptism taken on this work of carrying to God all the groaning of God's creation.

HOMILY IV

37

The bulletin insert on the next two pages can be reproduced, added to the parish bulletin or handed out after Mass. The shorter version that follows it can be typed into the bulletin if space is limited.

PEOPLE OF THE BOOK

A book can be a dangerous thing if people listen to it and live by it. To control people, the Nazis publicly burned books they did not like. They burned synagogues, too, and were especially interested in burning the Jews' sacred book — the Torah. A synagogue in Buffalo, New York, today uses a Torah scroll smuggled out of Nazi-occupied Czechoslovakia, saved by courageous Jews who risked their lives for their book.

A similar situation existed in the early church. In the second century, a Roman military leader wrote to his commander about a great disappointment he had when raiding a Christian church: His soldiers found and confiscated a stockpile of clothing (the church's collection for the poor), and some plates and cups (communion vessels), but they did not find what they really wanted — the book. Again, some brave believer risked everything to save the book.

So ever since the first days, we are people of the book. Our book is called the lectionary, because in it, most of the Bible is divided up into small portions (lections) to be read aloud when the church gathers to do anything important — baptize, confirm, witness a marriage, ordain, reconcile sinners, anoint the sick, bury the dead, celebrate Mass. We always open up our book and read from it before sharing the holy meal, and with the holy meal, the book makes us who we are: the word of God made flesh.

Our book is dangerous, though we may not know it. There are no Nazis or Romans beating at the door to burn it, but if we listen carefully to what our book tells us, and if we try to live by it, we may very well get into trouble. Our book challenges the way of the world. It asks "Why does might have to make right? Why does money matter most? Why do people have to be hungry, homeless and hopeless?"

Maybe we've grown too comfortable with our book. We treat it casually. We've heard it so many times that we barely listen to it any more. Homilies preached about what's in it sound like so much blah-blah-blah. What can we do?

First, we must listen. We must listen hard, and we must listen hard together. We must put aside the missalette and actively listen. Also, we have to pray that our readers and preachers do a good job, and expect — even demand — that they practice.

Next, we must ponder. We need a moment of silence after each of the first two readings and then after the homily. This is not free time. This is not time to read the bulletin or get money ready for the collection. This is time for us to ponder — to ponder hard and to ponder together in a communion of quiet.

Then will we begin to hear anew our dangerous book. Then will its words change us into something more than what we have been so far. Then, even though we may never have to risk our lives to smuggle our book to a safe place, we will still risk everything by carrying its message into our world. Then strange and wonderful things will happen.

Preaching about the Mass, © 1992 Archdiocese of Chicago, Liturgy Training Publications, 1800 North Hermitage Avenue, Chicago IL 60622-1101; 1-800-933-1800. Text by David Philippart. Design by Jill Smith.

PEOPLE OF THE BOOK

Christians are people of the book. Our book is called the lectionary, because in it, most of the Bible is divided up into small portions (lections) to be read aloud when the church gathers to do anything important. We always open up our book and read from it before sharing the holy meal, and with the holy meal, reading from the book makes us who we are: the word of God made flesh.

HOMILY IV

40

So we must listen. We must listen hard, and we must listen hard together. We must put aside the missalette and listen. This means that we also have to pray that our readers and preachers do a good job, and expect — demand — that they practice.

Next, we must ponder. We need a moment of silence after each of the first two readings and then again after the homily. This is not free time. This is not time to read the bulletin or get money ready for the collection. This is time for us to ponder — to ponder hard and to ponder together in a communion of quiet.

Then will we begin to hear our book anew. Then will it change us. Then will we carry God's word into our world.

Preaching about the Mass, © 1992 Archdiocese of Chicago, Liturgy Training Publications, 1800 North Hermitage Avenue, Chicago IL 60622-1101; 1-800-933-1800. Text by David Philippart. Design by Jill Smith.

REFLECTION QUESTIONS

1. What changes in yourself, your household, your neighborhood or your parish have come about as a result of hearing the scriptures proclaimed these past 25 years? What should be some of the effects of hearing the scriptures proclaimed week after week?

2. Does your parish observe the periods of silence after the readings? Are you comfortable during silence? How do you think we should use the silence after the readings? Before Mass, how do you prepare to hear the readings? After Mass, through the week, how do you mull over the readings?

3. Psalms are songs. Does your parish sing the psalms? Can you recall the words or melodies of psalm refrains? Words set to music can be easier to remember; perhaps that is one reason the psalms are better sung than spoken. Do you know any psalms by heart? The psalms are called a "school of prayer." They can teach us to pray. How can the parish help people learn the psalms?

4. The altar and the words of the gospel are kissed during the liturgy. What does that say about these things? Why are physical gestures important to the way we worship? How carefully do you make the gesture of welcoming the gospel by signing the forehead, the lips and the heart with the cross? Who taught it to you? Have you taught it to others?

5. The catechumens—the people preparing for baptism — are usually dismissed after the homily and before the creed. Who are these people in your parish? Why do only baptized people say the creed, pray the intercessions and then enter into the eucharist?

6. About the intercessions, the homily tells us, "Whatever else the church may be, it is an assembly that will not let God forget." How does your prayer throughout the week keep God in mind of the sufferings and troubles of this world?

HOMILY V

THE LITURGY OF THE EUCHARIST I

Every Sunday, every Lord's Day, the church assembles here in its house and processes into its liturgy. That procession we talked about a few weeks ago. There is our gathering together, song, the sign of the cross, greeting, prayer. It takes a while to give us a sense of being here not as so many individuals, but as the baptized people who are the church.

When this church has so prepared itself, we open our book and read the scriptures, sing psalms and alleluias, listen to the homily and join in the prayers of intercession. Those prayers conclude what is really a whole liturgy in itself, the liturgy of the word. But from their earliest times, Christians have had another liturgy that has been bound to their keeping of the Lord's day. That is the liturgy of the eucharist. "Eucharist" is a word that comes from Greek and has to do with "giving thanks," with "praise" and with "blessing."

But eucharist begins quietly. We need that. We have just finished what ought to be hard work; concentrating on the scripture and on making prayers of intercession takes energy and leaves us both lifted up and a little worn out. So we take quiet moments to get the room and ourselves ready for eucharist. This is the time called the preparation of the table or preparation of the gifts.

Bread and wine are brought forward, such simple things, food and drink associated with the tables of ordinary people. Here they are called "fruit of the earth" and "work of human hands" as they are placed on the table in our midst. At the same time, the "work of human hands" is seen in the money that is collected, money or other gifts that is explicitly called "for the church and the poor." Money could be collected in other ways and at other times; this is after all the age of credit cards. Why here and now? Because the money and the bread and wine are bound together. We are about to surround a single table and make a single prayer and eat of one bread and drink of one cup. Part of our preparation for this seems to be this gesture of pooling our resources, putting into one basket some of the money we have earned or received.

We get ready for eucharist by setting a table with bread and wine, but even more by showing some important things in this collection of money. One is that we are bound to one another — thus some of our contribution is for the work of the church. A second thing we show is that this bond is not selfish but is for the life of the world — thus some of our money is for the poor. And third, we show that what we do here together is bound to all the business and commerce and give-and-take of everyday life. Bread and wine show that, but perhaps money shows it even more clearly.

When all is ready, we stand up. In fact, we stand and gather around the table; only our numbers in this room keep us from coming into a circle. The one presiding stands at the table also and says four words to us that are not so much an invitation as an order: "Lift up your hearts." Some remember the Latin where it was only two words: *Sursum corda!* "Hearts on high!" we might say. And we answer that we are ready for this: "We lift them up to the Lord." Then the presider gives the invitation to do that deed that is the very heart not of the liturgy only but of Christian life: "Let us give thanks to the Lord our God." And we say: "It is right to give God thanks and praise." All right. It is. Giving thanks. Giving praise. That's the heart of things for us. Are we any good at it? Probably we are better at asking God, better at saying we're sorry, better at almost anything than this.

How do we think about those next few minutes? What do we think happens between this invitation and the Lord's Prayer just moments later? Some would say: "A lot of words by the priest while we all kneel down and pray." Others would say, "The priest consecrates the bread and wine." But there is a problem with answers like these. It still seems like we become a very passive audience right at the moment when we are supposed to be most active. The prayer that the presider speaks is the prayer of the church, our prayer. We show this when we sing those acclamations: "Holy, holy, holy Lord, God of power and might," and "Christ has died, Christ is risen," and the Great Amen that we sing at the end of this prayer. All of those are shouts of approval, commands to go ahead with this prayer. They are like bursts of single-hearted song.

Or are they? Sometimes they are not. Part of that may be our fault, part the presider's fault, part the fault of words that are not strong enough to bear the burden here, and part the fault of music that just doesn't get the job done for us. All of those can be improved. Our failure to make these moments the high point of the liturgy shows that the liturgy is very human. It isn't magic. From the presider's side, it takes great strength to lead the eucharistic prayer well, speaking a long prayer to God in the name of this assembly. A person can't do that without sensing that the assembly is attentive, is wanting to give thanks and praise.

That back-and-forth between the leader of the prayer and the ones praying is crucial. Posture, eyes, readiness to sing those acclamations — all these count. Despite an unfortunate distance between the leader and the assembly, we can get rid of all papers and books and have eyes and all senses toward the table. We can sing out, by heart, the "Holy, holy" and the other acclamations. Though the spoken words of the prayer are familiar, we can try to hear them and make them our own prayer so that our "Amen" is real at the end.

Though there are in English nine different forms that this prayer can take, each weaves together some common strands. Most obvious: This is a meal prayer. God is given all thanks and praise, not in the abstract but at a table on which are the bread and wine intended for the food and drink of this assembly. So this prayer echoes with all the meal blessings we say in our lives. We grow hungry and by God's grace are fed. All that we know about giving thanks, we bring to this table. Over the bread and wine the presider puts words to our thanks, and they become words about Christ. All our thanks gravitate toward the body given up for the life of the world, toward the blood of the new and everlasting covenant, blood that was shed for all that sins might be forgiven. We call on the Holy Spirit to come on these gifts and make them holy, make them for us the body and blood of our Lord, Jesus Christ.

HOMILY V

46

If we Catholics want to learn how to pray, then let us learn how to pray the eucharistic prayer. Learn how to lift up our hearts and give God thanks and praise. Learn it here, at this table, gathered close to one another, gazing at simple bread and good wine.

The bulletin insert on the next two pages can be reproduced, added to the parish bulletin or handed out after Mass. The shorter version that follows it can be typed into the bulletin if space is limited.

ALWAYS THANKSGIVING

The liturgy of the eucharist refers to the part of the Mass that begins with the collection and the preparation of the altar and the bread and wine. What are we doing in these actions? Much of the answer lies in the word "eucharist." Derived from the Greek, it means "thanksgiving."

Our thanksgiving is best expressed in the main prayer of the liturgy of the eucharist, the eucharistic prayer. Some history of this prayer: Its roots are in the Jewish tradition of meal blessings. As a devout Jew, Jesus would have prayed such blessings at meals. Early Christians (who were Jews) used them in their celebrations known as "the breaking of the bread," when they obeyed Jesus' command to "Do this in memory of me." Over time, references to Jesus and the meaning of his life, death and resurrection were incorporated into these blessings. Two of the nine eucharistic prayers we now use date from the third and fourth centuries, and the other seven are recent compositions. All follow a similar pattern. In other words, Christians have been praying this way at the eucharist ever since there were Christians!

The eucharistic prayer is thanksgiving for the heart of life as Christians understand it: for all of God's creation, and especially for the saving works of Christ. It is proclaimed over bread and wine, symbols of what is most basic, food and drink from the tables of ordinary people. In this context, when we are focused on the foundations of our life, we also petition God for the abundance promised at this table to be shared with the whole world, with the church, with all who seek God, with the dead.

The prayer is an action that everyone in the church is meant to participate in: It is not "the priest's prayer." This idea is new to many Catholics. From "The Lord be with you" and the dialogue that follows, through the Great Amen, the eucharistic prayer requires the vigorous participation of all present. We involve ourselves fully when we join our hearts to the words sung or spoken by the priest, when we assume an attentive posture, when we put aside the missalette and listen, when we sing the acclamations with full voice.

In the end, "eucharist" is what our life as Christians is all about. Wherever we stand, in suffering or joy or confusion or routine, our life is always to be thanksgiving, always to be a sharing of God's abundance with all in need.

Preaching about the Mass, © 1992 Archdiocese of Chicago, Liturgy Training Publications, 1800 North Hermitage Avenue, Chicago IL 60622-1101; 1-800-933-1800. Text by Elizabeth Hoffman. Design by Jill Smith.

ALWAYS THANKSGIVING

The eucharistic prayer ("eucharist" means "thanksgiving"), beginning with "The Lord be with you" and ending with the Great Amen, is the central part of the Mass. It is proclaimed over the bread and wine, basic symbols of life and death. We praise God for all creation and for the saving life, death and resurrection of Jesus — such praise requires the participation of all present; it is not the priest's prayer. We involve ourselves fully when we join our hearts to the words sung or spoken, assume an attentive posture, put aside the missalette and sing the acclamations with full voice.

HOMILY V

49

  In the end, "eucharist" is what our life as Christians is all about. In suffering or joy or confusion or routine, our life is always to be praise, always to be thanksgiving, always to be a sharing of God's abundance with all in need.

Preaching about the Mass, © 1992 Archdiocese of Chicago, Liturgy Training Publications, 1800 North Hermitage Avenue, Chicago IL 60622-1101; 1-800-933-1800. Text by Elizabeth Hoffman. Design by Jill Smith.

REFLECTION QUESTIONS

1. What does the parish's communion bread look like and taste like and smell like? (After all, bread really should have a wonderful aroma.) Who bakes it? From where does the wine come? Why is it important to know?

2. What is the eucharistic prayer of the Mass — with what does it begin and with what does it end? Why is this prayer so important? Does it sound and feel important as it is prayed in your parish? Does this prayer enable you to offer God your praise and thanksgiving? How does a person "learn to pray the eucharistic prayer"?

3. For an exercise, spend some time reading over the eucharistic prayers of the church. To whom are they addressed? Here is where the church remembers and gives thanks for God's gifts; here, too, the church makes its offering and calls on God's Spirit to come and bind us in communion. In the various eucharistic prayers, identify the words of remembrance, of self-sacrifice and of the unity of the Spirit.

HOMILY V

50

4. The Orthodox theologian Alexander Schmemann wrote that in the liturgy we "ascend into mystery." Of course, that's just what we proclaim in the prefaces of the eucharistic prayers. The "Holy, holy" makes clear into whose presence we have ascended. How on earth can we prepare to stand alongside the company of heaven?

5. The thought of ascending into heaven each time we offer the eucharist can take our breath away. A prerequisite for entering into the mystery of Christ is a willingness to lay down our lives for each other. How can this awesome sacrifice be made evident at worship? (There can be countless answers to this question.)

HOMILY VI

THE LITURGY OF THE EUCHARIST II

Every Sunday, we celebrate — this church celebrates — the eucharist. We gather, we read the scriptures together, we make prayers of intercession, then we gather gifts for the poor and the church and we prepare the table with our bread and wine. Around the table, we join in speaking and singing thanksgiving for all God's gifts, all gifts gathered in the body of Christ given for us, the blood of Christ that is shed for the forgiveness of sins. To all of this we give our firm assent, our Amen. The presider concludes, "...all glory and honor is yours...for ever and ever." Amen! The eucharistic prayer depends on and ends with this Amen. We say Amen. To say Amen is our duty and our right, as this people who died in baptism and live now in Christ. It is our right; it is our duty.

So then we are ready for that part of the liturgy we call communion, holy communion. After that Amen, we pray the dearest, hardest prayer we know, the Lord's Prayer. This prayer rightly comes in many places in our lives. It is a morning and a night prayer for many. It is a prayer at bedside and at graveside. Here it is a communion prayer. Recited or sung, it is everyone's prayer, the words we all own. And still they are the words that we never will own. What can it mean to pray that God's name be hallowed, be holy? What kind of courage and longing does it take to pray that God's will be done?

In the eucharistic prayer, the assembly and the presider pray in a sort of dialogue; the affirmations and acclamations of the people flow back and forth with the words spoken by the presider. But when we come to the Lord's Prayer, we take the leading role ourselves, we the assembly, the people. We pray the Lord's Prayer together, then exchange the greeting of peace, and go on to the Lamb of God litany. All — Lord's

Prayer, peace greeting, Lamb of God — take us to the communion procession itself.

What sort of moment is the peace greeting? Why, after being together all this time, would we turn to one another and embrace or shake hands? Perhaps it is that, moments before we share the bread and wine, we give a sign for what that communion means. We turn to one and all alike and say, "Peace," or "Christ's peace." The communion means no walls. It means no first place and last place but all in the same place. It means today is God's reign, some little bit of it, here, among us. This goes beyond the hospitality we extend to one another on arriving for the liturgy. It is caught up in this word "peace," the greeting spoken by the risen Lord to the disciples. To say "peace" and to clasp hands or to embrace others is physically laying down whatever keeps us from communion with one another. Some of the people near us may be family, some may be friends, some will be strangers: We have the same word, gaze and unity with all.

When we have extended this peace to one another, we slowly focus back toward the table. There, our ministers of communion have gathered with the presider, ready to prepare this tiny meal we call a banquet. The presider takes up the bread and breaks it for all to see. This simple gesture is, in a sense, only doing what must be done so that the bread can be shared with all present. But it is the single act that the early Christians fastened on; the name they gave to their Sunday assemblies was "the breaking of the bread." That act of taking a large loaf of bread and breaking it into pieces caught the essence of their gathering. Here was the one and the many; here was Christ of whom they were all members.

As the bread is broken and divided into serving dishes and as the wine is poured into cups, we sing a litany. The first words are "Lamb of God," and the response sung by all is "have mercy on us." The communion procession itself may begin during this litany, this breaking of the bread.

When all is ready for the communion, the final words we sing are "Grant us peace," and immediately the one presiding invites all to the table with these words: "This is the Lamb of God." And we say, "Lord, I am not worthy." And we are not. No one is. But that is exactly why we so need to come forward to eat and to drink the body and blood of Christ.

Do you see how it all depends on us, on all who gather in this room, and not simply on the priest? The priest is our leader of prayer and our servant. We are the ones who must do these rites of Lord's Prayer and Peace, Lamb of God and now communion. There is no audience. None. All are partakers because it is the loving deed of the church that gets done here, and no other.

And so we come forward. We who are hungry and thirsty come forward to the table. We fast before Mass because to be here at all is to be hungry and thirsty in our hearts and minds and even our bodies. This procession that we make is not like going to the bank or the supermarket. At those places we just line up. But here, this is a procession. It is a procession to a common meal of a common people on the earthy food of bread and the earthy drink of wine become for us the body and the blood of Christ our Lord. It is a procession, and it must look and move and feel like a procession. That is why we sing through this time. It is the music of moving as one, as the church.

When we stand one by one before the minister and hear the words, "The body of Christ," "The blood of Christ," we have to know what Augustine told his congregation hundreds of years ago. He said, "It is your own mystery that you receive. Say Amen to what you are!" Say Amen to what you are: the body of Christ. The blood of Christ. Come with hands extended, look at the communion minister as she or he looks at you and says, "The body of Christ," "The blood of Christ." Say Amen, yes, this — this bread, this person, this people: the body of Christ. Amen.

Jesus said, "Take and eat, all of you." Jesus said, "Take and drink, all of you." So we do that. The cup is not an extra for those who like extras. It is what Jesus told us to do. Take the cup in your hands and drink from it. It is the taste of the heavenly banquet. It is Jesus there for our every thirst. If I am disconnected from my child or friend, physically or emotionally, I thirst. If I am in grief or full of cares, I thirst. If I have failed at work or if my work goes unrecognized, I thirst. If I am one with this struggling and suffering world, I must thirst. We are a thirsty church and this is Jesus, this cup of the covenant, Jesus for whom we thirst. And this cup is also to be our bond of delight in this church and world that are so often not delightful at all.

All through the communion of this church, all through it, let our prayer be the singing of the church, let our posture be attentive and alive. And when the great procession is over, then there can be a great silence, a needed time for contemplation of this wonder. In silence, too, we are in communion. We ponder together that there is indeed food for our hunger and there is drink for our thirst.

So this time together, after the liturgy of the word, is a lot like a meal where we meet around a table, give thanks for all God's goodness, and have our hunger and thirst satisfied for the moment. It is hunger not only of the body but for communion with each other. We need to know such meals in our daily life so that we might know the renewal and refreshment and the sacrifice, too, the all-embracing sacrifice, of this Sunday meal as the church.

A quiet prayer concludes our communion. Then we hear the "announcements" which are the business of this community. We share the blessing, say "Thanks be to God" to words of departure and, on most occasions, join in song as we prepare to take leave of one another.

To have a liturgy that lets us pour out our whole lives as Christians and that gives us strength and challenge to live all the hours of the week as Christians, we who are this assembly, we the people who surround the book and who surround the table, must ourselves take on the hard work that is the church's — making praise of our God.

The bulletin insert on the next two pages can be reproduced, added to the parish bulletin or handed out after Mass. The shorter version that follows it can be typed into the bulletin if space is limited.

HOMILY VI

57

YES, IT IS SO!

We've sung the Great Amen, finished the eucharistic prayer, and are moving toward communion. What's happening at this time of the Mass?

We begin with the Lord's Prayer, the prayer all Christians share, the prayer that marks all kinds of moments. Here, it is a sign of communion, words that we all can say or sing by heart. From this part of the Mass onward, it is especially clear that what we are doing is *our* doing, and not simply the priest's. The words of the Lord's Prayer belong to all of us. They sum up the basics of our life: praising God's holiness, praying for the reign of God, asking for our daily bread.

From the Lord's Prayer we move closer to communion. We exchange a sign of peace. It is far more than a "warm fuzzy" moment among intimates. A handshake or a hug, offered to family, friend and stranger, adult and child — we say by this action that there are no walls, that the reign of God is among us now.

Our focus returns to the table. The body of Christ is broken for all, the blood of Christ poured out for all. We sing the Lamb of God litany, praising Christ over and over for taking away our sins, begging again and again for mercy and for peace.

We begin to move to the table, our communion procession. We sing at this time, another sign that we are one body. Here, in a morsel of bread and a sip of wine is a feast to satisfy our deepest hunger and thirst. *Our* deepest hunger and thirst — mine, yes, but my neighbor's, too, and indeed the whole world's.

When the minister places the piece of bread or the cup in our hands and says "The body of Christ," "The blood of Christ," we say "Amen." That Amen means "Yes, it is so;

Yes, I believe." St. Augustine told his congregation something else about the Amen: "It is your own mystery you receive. Say Amen to what you are!" What you are — the body and blood of Christ. Our Amen sends us forth to live as Christ's body and blood in our homes, our schools, our workplaces, our neighborhoods, our world.

Preaching about the Mass, © 1992 Archdiocese of Chicago, Liturgy Training Publications, 1800 North Hermitage Avenue, Chicago IL 60622-1101; 1-800-933-1800. Text by Elizabeth Hoffman. Design by Jill Smith.

YES, IT IS SO!

Several actions surround the sharing of communion. We begin with the Lord's Prayer, a prayer we know by heart, the prayer that sums up the basics of our life: praising God's holiness, praying for God's reign, asking for daily bread. We exchange a greeting of peace, a sign that God's reign is among us, shared with friend and stranger alike. We sing the Lamb of God as Christ's body is broken and his blood poured out, and move to the table to commune with Christ and each other. In this tiny meal, a fragment of bread and a sip of wine, our deepest hunger and thirst are satisfied. We say Amen, and by that Amen, promise to live as the body and blood of Christ, in our homes, schools, workplaces, neighborhoods — in our world.

Preaching about the Mass, © 1992 Archdiocese of Chicago, Liturgy Training Publications, 1800 North Hermitage Avenue, Chicago IL 60622-1101; 1-800-933-1800. Text by Elizabeth Hoffman. Design by Jill Smith.

REFLECTION QUESTIONS

1. "Thy kingdom come; thy will be done..." are for many people hard and strong words of prayer. Other than the eucharist, when do you pray the Lord's Prayer? Why is it the right prayer before communion?

2. How well does the way in which your parish extends the greeting of peace enact these words: "Some of the people near us may be family, some may be friends, some will be strangers: We have the same word, gaze and unity with all"?

3. It takes knowledge and thought and rehearsal to do the communion rite well according to the ritual requirements of our tradition and according to the needs of the parish and the limitations of the building. Overall, there should be a calmness and a graciousness to most everyone's movement and actions. How can this be accomplished in your parish?

4. Many of the traditional actions at communion have deep meaning. For example, according to our tradition someone hands us the bread and cup when we receive communion; we don't simply help ourselves from the altar. What does this signify? What might it mean to break and share a single loaf and share a common cup?

5. "We are a thirsty church." Communion from the cup is a relatively new thing to many of us. In more and more parishes it is becoming not an option but an essential part of the way everyone shares communion. How have you come to appreciate better Jesus' commandment, "Take this, all of you, and drink from it"?

6. What ordinarily do you do after Sunday Mass? How do you keep the rest of the day holy? Under ideal circumstances, how do you think you would like to keep Sundays? What steps can you take to move toward your ideals? Do you see and mingle and perhaps pray with parishioners during the week? How can you make connections between worship on Sundays and your work throughout the week?

HOMILY VI

61

HOMILY VII

When preachers and musicians argue about whether the homily or the music is the most important part of the liturgy, the musicians always have the last word. Usually they say, "No one ever left church on Sunday humming the homily."

And they are right. What we sing here on Sundays has a way of getting into our souls. Once we recognize that the Sunday Mass is not something that we watch but something that we do, all of us, then we ask: How? How can we say that 40 or 400 or 1400 persons in a room around a book and a table can all be the ones that make this liturgy?

Song is one of the answers to that. Perhaps it is the first answer. We come here and we assemble and then we have a choice of how we understand every song that comes from us. Some would observe what goes on here and say: Well, yes, the ritual takes place, and now and then we stop and sing a song or maybe we sing as background while something else is taking place. That's one way to explain our singing here.

The other way to understand what happens here is this: The people assembled here, all of us, sing our liturgy. The liturgy isn't something that stops so we can insert a song; it isn't something we can add singing to as background music. Rather, the liturgy is something people sing. Singing is one way we can say that this liturgy is done by everyone here. It isn't something extra, something to make things longer or more solemn. Our singing is us doing the liturgy. It is the church doing what the church needs to do.

We Catholics who are old enough remember the days of high Mass and low Mass. High Mass had singing, though not often by all the people. Sometimes one person played the organ and sang all the parts. Sometimes a choir learned elaborate settings of the words. And then there was low Mass with no singing. When the bishops of the world at Vatican Council II began the renewal of the liturgy, they did away with this distinction. Singing was to be restored to the people at every Sunday Mass. The past 25 years have witnessed many efforts to give song to the people, but it has clearly been difficult. Lots of people went off in lots of directions. Many well-intentioned but sometimes silly things have been written and sung. But much has been learned also, and there is need now to get on with the challenge.

Why is it challenging for us? Why don't we want to get in here and raise the roof with our songs? I can think of two reasons for starters.

First, we Americans don't sing; we hire people to do our singing for us. Thanks to the amplifier, the Walkman and Muzak, we have music in our ears more than any people ever. But we don't have it in our throats. We listen. We're the audience. Just walking through these church doors doesn't change that. Song has been woven thoroughly into the ordinary lives of ordinary people through most of human history. We have had work songs, holiday songs, lullabies, love songs, campfire songs, political songs, children's nursery-rhyme songs and jump rope songs, protest songs, patriotic songs. These have been songs for the people, for us. But there isn't much of any of that any more. So we come here cold. We come here expecting someone else to do the singing. And that is a terrible clash. No one else can sing the Mass for us. If we won't do it, all of us together, it won't be done.

A second reason then that makes singing here such a challenge: We believe, deep down, that it really doesn't matter if "I" sing or not. How could it matter what I do? I'm just the person on the end of the 19th pew. I may be one who slips in and out without a word to anyone, or I may really look forward to gathering here with people I know.

Both challenges affect all of us. We're not used to being singers; we like to listen. We're not used to thinking of ourselves as the ones responsible for the liturgy; we just come to pray. No amount of urging, demanding, begging, is going to change that for a lot of us.

Maybe all that can change it is good experience. To be even once in the midst of an assembly of people who sing with delight and from their hearts can open the eyes — and the mouth. Suddenly I know what song is meant to be, a way that diverse human beings can have solidarity with one another. Suddenly I know that this gathering isn't about my praying — that can go on all week — it is about the church praying, and the prayer of this church is louder and softer than any speaking voice; it needs to hold onto sounds longer or let sounds go more quickly than any speaking voice.

When we have the experience each Sunday of a liturgy sung by all, we know without anything being said that this song of the church takes many sounds and that we need all of them. We need the short songs like the Alleluia and the "Holy, holy," and the Great Amen. Songs like these are how a crowd of people can make the church's prayer; we don't all have to say everything, but we all sing our agreement and our praise.

We, the church, need songs where our part is just to repeat the same thing over and over, litanies where we sing "Lord, have mercy," or "Have mercy on us," or "Hear our prayer." These shape us into the church, the people on this earth who were marked by baptism to watch out for all the troubles and sorrows and demand God's mercy.

We, the church, need those songs like the one we sing each Sunday after the first reading, the psalms from the Bible. These are our first songs and our last songs. They are the songs that teach us everything about how we sing. They are so old and from a culture that was hardly anything like ours, but that is just where they are great: They are what binds us to our ancestors and to one another. They are hard for us to take, but take them we must.

And we, the church, need all those other songs that are the poetry of the church through the centuries and today, the hymns and spirituals and carols, the poetry set to music in so many styles of singing. From old hymns from the Latin like "O come, O come, Emmanuel" or "Pange lingua," to distinctly American songs like "Precious Lord, take my hand," or "What wondrous love," to modern compositions which may or may not stand the test of time. This is our music for going in and going out on Sundays, music that often teaches more than theology books do about what being a Christian means.

In the end, Catholics are human beings and human beings have known for a long time that they leave the ordinary speaking voice at the door when they come to do the things that matter most in life. What we know that makes singing even more vital for us is this: When we come through these doors, what we do we do as the church. Singing — where the voice of the individual is taken up in the voice of the assembly — is how the church does what it must do and delights to do: the repentance, the praise, the thanks, the intercession that is the singing voice of Christ in this world.

The bulletin insert on the next two pages can be reproduced, added to the parish bulletin or handed out after Mass. The shorter version that follows it can be typed into the bulletin if space is limited.

RECITING "HAPPY BIRTHDAY"

Imagine this: You're at a baseball game, and the two teams are announced and take their places. Then the announcer asks that all stand and join in *reciting* the national anthem. What would that be like? Try this: The next time you're at a birthday gathering, suggest that instead of singing "Happy Birthday" that all present *say* it. Does it work?

Probably not. Certain moments in life *need* song. Reciting "Happy Birthday" instead of singing it somehow weakens the good wishes and lessens the love that the simple song communicates. Singing the simple melody — and singing it *together* — that's what is important. Singing doesn't just dress up the words, it gives them meaning.

Traditionally, human beings turn to song at the high points and low points of their lives. Song makes both joy and sorrow bearable. All human cultures except maybe our own have thus had traditional songs to sing on the happiest occasions and the saddest. Today, we turn to song at the happiest and saddest moments of our lives, too. But we rarely sing. Instead we turn on the stereo and listen. We have songs for parties, songs to listen to while we clean the house, songs we listen to when we are sad and songs we listen to when wondering what life is all about.

Listening to music is good. The problem is that we are so accustomed to listening that we don't sing. So when we come to church, we come to listen and not to sing. Yet Mass is meant to be sung. It is one of those moments in life that requires song to express its deepest meaning. It limps as badly as a recited "Happy Birthday" when it is not sung.

It is important that everyone sing at Mass, too. While there are parts of the Mass that certain individuals sing — the priest chants the preface of the eucharistic prayer or the cantor sings the verses of the responsorial psalm, for example — the majority of the sung parts belong to all of us. We sing acclamations: "Alleluia!" "Holy, holy, holy Lord!" "Amen!" We sing litanies: "Lord, have mercy!" "Hear our prayer!" "Grant us peace!" We sing hymns, spirituals, canticles and carols.

And in all this singing something wonderful happens. Many voices blend and become one. A communion of singers occurs. Have you ever been outside a room or building wherein people were singing? As you listen, can you tell how many there are? You may be able to tell if it is a big group or a small one, but you can't judge with any certainty if it is five or fifty. You can't tell because how ever many voices there are, in song they become one.

St. Augustine said that one of the things that convinced him to convert to Christ was the strong singing of the Alleluia that he heard coming from the liturgical assembly. That singing lured him in and changed his life forever. Can the same be said of our parish's singing? If not, resolve to sing louder and with more spirit next Sunday.

Preaching about the Mass, © 1992 Archdiocese of Chicago, Liturgy Training Publications, 1800 North Hermitage Avenue, Chicago IL 60622-1101; 1-800-933-1800. Text by David Philippart. Design by Jill Smith.

RECITING "HAPPY BIRTHDAY"

The Mass is meant to be sung. It is one of those moments in life that requires song to express its deepest meaning. It limps as badly as a recited "Happy Birthday" when it is not sung by all.

It is important that everyone sing at Mass. While there are parts of the Mass that certain individuals sing — the priest chants the preface of the eucharistic prayer or the cantor sings the verses of the responsorial psalm, for example — the majority of the sung parts belong to all of us. We sing acclamations: "Alleluia!" "Holy, holy, holy Lord!" "Amen!" We sing litanies: "Lord, have mercy!" "Hear our prayer!" "Grant us peace!" We sing hymns, spirituals, canticles and carols.

And in all this singing something wonderful happens. Many voices blend and become one. A communion of singers occurs. Be part of the communion. Lift up your voice next Sunday. Sing loud and with spirit.

Preaching about the Mass, © 1992 Archdiocese of Chicago, Liturgy Training Publications, 1800 North Hermitage Avenue, Chicago IL 60622-1101; 1-800-933-1800. Text by David Philippart. Design by Jill Smith.

REFLECTION QUESTIONS

1. Name a few songs you know by heart. Do you do much singing with friends or relatives, or by yourself? It's not likely that congregational singing will be all it can be unless folks learn the joys of singing at times other than at worship. What can the parish do to encourage singing at home?

2. The homily calls the psalms "our first songs and our last songs." How can we help make the psalms songs we sing by heart, from the heart, wholeheartedly?

3. Have you ever experienced being in a roomful of people singing with gusto? What was the occasion and what did you sing? Were you accompanied by instruments? If yes, could you hear them? Not only in your ears but even in your skin, what did it feel like to be surrounded with sound?

4. People can be taught to sing. It's an acquired skill. And, like any skill, singing is best learned step by step, in lessons, and not haphazardly. Because singing is the way we worship as a community, what is the parish doing to teach the skills of singing, especially to the young?

5. Spoken worship would be regarded as downright strange by most of the world's peoples. The homily gives a few reasons why we as a people don't sing as much as we once did. Why do you think we are accustomed to speaking instead of singing our praise?

6. Are you comfortable with the sound of your singing voice? Most people would not be comfortable singing a solo. That's the best thing about being in a crowd of singers — your own voice gets blended in. Does the seating arrangement in your church help this happen? Carpeting or drapery or ceiling tiles that were installed to make a church more comfortable can deaden sound and make communal singing difficult. What can be done to improve the acoustics of the church?

HOMILY VIII

You just sat down. That movement is part of the liturgy. So, in fact, is what I am doing: Standing to address you. In our culture, sitting isn't just the restful posture, it is also the receptive posture. And standing isn't just the posture of the person who has nowhere to sit, it is the active and engaged posture.

People can't get away from posture. When a few of us or a lot of us come together for a common ritual, our postures play an even larger part. Posture is a sort of language.

This language is not the "body language" people spoke much of some years back (if I cross my arms when I'm talking to you it means I'm not really involved in the conversation any more). This is body language, but it is a language we memorize, know by heart and generally do together.

If we want to understand something about posture's language at the liturgy and why it matters, it helps to look at how we learn to use various postures in various groups for various occasions. For instance, what has our culture made of the act of standing up? You're at the ballpark and they begin the "Star-spangled Banner." You're in a courtroom and the judge rises to leave the bench. You are sitting at a mortuary visiting with friends and the widow of the deceased comes into the room and over to your group. You're back at the ballpark, the home team is losing by a run in the bottom of the ninth, there is a runner on second and two out. What posture do you assume?

We get to our feet: for the judge, for the national anthem, for the widow, for the — we hope — base hit to tie the game or home run to win it outright. It isn't just habit and it isn't just emotion, but habit and emotion have something to do with it. It is the meaning standing gives to the moment and the meaning the moment gives to standing.

Another culture might say that bowing over or kneeling was the right response for one or all of these moments. There is something arbitrary after all about this, an agreement that we enter into: To us, standing seems to mean just this and that — but we can see how other tribes on the earth could come to see these same things expressed in a completely different posture.

For us, standing can't be pinned down to just one little meaning: respect, say, or attention. It takes in a variety of related attitudes. At Sunday Mass, we stand to enter into the liturgy. We stand at the first approach of the gospel proclamation. We stand — ordinarily — to make our prayers of intercession. We are on our feet again when we are urged by the presider to lift up our hearts and give thanks to the Lord our God. And we stand to go out from the room and our liturgy. For us, these are the moments that call for a posture that is engaged, ready to act, a posture that manifests respect and shows great attention to the matter at hand. People growing up and growing old in this culture probably would feel a little uncomfortable sitting during the procession that begins our liturgy or kneeling during the proclamation of the gospel.

Think of how we use the notion of standing in our English expressions. We say that a person stands on their own two feet. We stand up to be counted. We stand for something. We stand by each other. In an old Latin expression, ancient Christians called themselves the "circumstantes." This meant that they were the people who "stand around" or, better, the people who "stand in a circle." That is how they saw themselves, a community of people standing around the altar, encircling the altar. Today, that is this community. We are the people who "stand around" the altar, who stand to surround the altar. For nearly all of the church's history, there have been no chairs, no pews, no benches. This is how it continues throughout many of the world's Christian churches. Perhaps the standing posture, so much more active than sitting, serves well to teach us what being in this room means.

Standing is about respect, about attention, about readiness. For us, it is the basic posture, the normal posture. Anything else is a temporary departure, a little sitting, a little kneeling, then we get back to our basic "stance."

If we sit down during the liturgy, it is usually to allow us to listen more attentively or to reflect in silence without the distraction of bearing all our weight on our two feet. Sitting is good for those tasks, but it has major drawbacks in that we can let it become the posture of an audience, and that is what we are not.

Likewise, the kneeling posture for us has associations with repentance and with penance, with an attitude that expresses adoration, and sometimes simply with the posture an individual wants to take in moments of private prayer. For most of the history of the church, the people didn't sit down — pews were only widely used after the Reformation. And kneeling was done by Catholics in the liturgy itself only at rare moments. Now we can say that sitting and kneeling are part of how Catholic communities in this society do the liturgy, each has a certain limited place. But still, it should feel to us as Catholics that when we come together to do the liturgy, we do it on our feet.

Do we think of standing as our basic posture here? That's hard when so much of the furniture in this room is about sitting. It puts us in the mind to watch — passively. It can make us feel like prisoners, walled in before and behind by heavy furniture, lined up in rows. But we really are those *circumstantes*, those who stand around the table. This is Christ's banquet table in our midst, this altar, but our banquet is a banquet of pilgrims. The food here is the bread and wine eaten by those on a journey. It is a glimpse of a banquet, a glimpse of what we are moving toward—but we are people on the move, on our feet, not yet at ease.

A priest told me once about weddings: "I've had it with these people at weddings, Catholics who act as though they haven't been to Mass for years. They have no idea when to sit or kneel or stand. I used to tell them: Please be seated. Please stand. Please kneel. Then one day when I was fuming about it all, I thought: Wait a minute. Don't they have some responsibility? Why do I have to know my part and they don't have to know theirs? So, now I never tell them anything. If they sit the whole time, fine. If they kneel for the entire wedding, fine."

That sounds harsh, but there's a strong point. Posture here is not arbitrary. It isn't just anything the leader wants to make it. It isn't whatever you feel like at the moment. It is the posture we take, not as individuals but as the church. So here are not two hundred and fifty individuals standing up, here is the vigilant, watchful, active body of believers. Our standing tells us what sort of church we are. Thus it shows respect and it teaches us respect: respect for one another as God's creatures and as members of the body of Christ, and respect that springs from the presence of Christ in the word proclaimed from scripture and in bread and wine. Likewise, our standing here is a rehearsal for how we mean to be when we leave here: engaged with the world and one another, alert for God's kingdom, standing firm, standing in solidarity with brothers and sisters.

To sit down with this assembly is also a rehearsal. It isn't like sitting in a theater or before the TV or on the porch after a day's work. It isn't sitting to relax or be entertained. This is sitting to hear the lector read the scriptures to the church. It is sitting to let silence wash over us as we pray and reflect. Little by little, this posture teaches us how to listen and what to listen for. Little by little, the sitting we do here makes us a contemplative people, a people who can keep prayer rolling around inside us even in the busiest times of our daily living.

And to kneel with this assembly during penitential or very intense times is also a rehearsing. We need to be people who know what it means to be on our knees in sadness and sorrow, in adoration, in daily night prayers for forgiveness and for peace. Our worship here, Sunday by Sunday, is not only in the words of prayers and songs, it is in the whole human person that we are here. How each one of us joins in the liturgy — kneeling, sitting and standing — that is what makes and shapes and hammers out this liturgy of word and eucharist, the work and the delight given us at baptism.

HOMILY VIII

77

The bulletin insert on the next two pages can be reproduced, added to the parish bulletin or handed out after Mass. The shorter version that follows it can be typed into the bulletin if space is limited.

OUR BODIES JOIN IN PRAISE

Mass is more than words: Our whole body is involved in our greatest act of praise and thanks to God. We stand, we sit, we bow, we kneel, we raise our hands to heaven, we process, we cup one hand within the other to receive a morsel of bread, we take hold of a cup to drink. These postures are second nature to most of us; it's only after a wedding or funeral when a non-Catholic friend asks "Why are you Catholics always up and down at your service?" that we are aware of how our bodies join in the liturgy. The question of why is a good one, though.

Why do we stand at Mass? We stand to begin. We stand to welcome the gospel and to listen to it carefully. We stand to make intercession before God for the needs of the world and the church. In some places, we stand during the great prayer of thanksgiving, the eucharistic prayer. We stand to eat the Lord's body and drink his blood. Finally, we stand to take leave of our assembly. Why?

Standing in our culture is a sign of respect. We stand when someone important enters the room. We stand when we are introduced to a new person. We stand when the national anthem is sung. Standing is also a sign of attention —we "stand guard." Standing means we are ready to move. We stand up sometimes to say that this visit or this conversation is ending now, and it's time to move on. We "stand around" and wait for someone so we can go together.

So it is only natural that we stand when we do at Mass. We show respect for the gathered assembly. We show respect for the gospel. We show respect for God when we ask for things in the prayers of the faithful (and also stand ready to serve as part of God's answer to those prayers). We eat and drink the eucharist standing—actually processing—because like the Israelites who were told by God to eat their meal with their shoes and coats on and their walking sticks in hand, we are people on a journey, traveling through this life to the Promised Land. We stand to end our liturgy because we are told that the reason we gathered in the first place was to be able to "go in peace to love and serve the Lord."

Why do we sit at Mass? We sit for the readings and the homily. We sit for the preparation of the gifts and a moment of silence after communion. Why? We sit so we can listen and be attentive. We "take the load off of our feet" in order to ponder. But we must be careful that our sitting doesn't lull us to sleep. In our culture we sit when we want to be passive, or entertained. We sit to watch television. We're quiet then, but not involved much. That's not the kind of sitting liturgy needs.

Why do we kneel? We kneel sometimes to beg for mercy or to ask the saints to pray for us or the Holy Spirit to come down upon us. Why? Kneeling is the posture of a servant, of someone in need. We are both before God.

Our postures are an important part of our prayer. Let's use them with care at Mass and in our prayer at home, too.

Preaching about the Mass, © 1992 Archdiocese of Chicago, Liturgy Training Publications, 1800 North Hermitage Avenue, Chicago IL 60622-1101, 1-800-933-1800. Text by David Philippart. Design by Jill Smith.

OUR BODIES JOIN IN PRAISE

Mass is more than words: Our whole body is involved in our greatest act of praise and thanks to God. We stand, we sit, we bow, we kneel, we raise our hands to heaven, we process, we cup one hand within the other to receive a morsel of bread, we take hold of a cup to drink. Why?

Standing is a sign of respect: We stand when someone important enters the room, or when we meet a person. So it's natural that we stand to show respect for the gathered assembly or the gospel. We stand to show respect when we ask God for the needs of the world and church in the prayers of the faithful, and we stand ready to be part of God's answer to those prayers. We stand to eat and drink the eucharist because we are pilgrims on the road to the Promised Land, taking nourishment on the way.

Similarly we sit in order to listen better. And we kneel because kneeling is what a servant does, and we are God's servants. Posture is an important part of our prayer as Catholics. Let's stand, sit and kneel with care.

Preaching about the Mass, © 1992 Archdiocese of Chicago, Liturgy Training Publications, 1800 North Hermitage Avenue, Chicago IL 60622-1101; 1-800-933-1800. Text by David Philippart. Design by Jill Smith.

REFLECTION QUESTIONS

1. In the homily is a short list of times when people stand up. Can you add to the list? What gestures do you use when greeting or leaving others? Why are gestures of courtesy and respect and affection important?

2. If a visitor to your home didn't first remove her or his coat and hat, what would that say about the visit? What are the ways you make yourself "at home" when coming to worship? Some parishes have installed coat closets so people can worship unencumbered by winter gear. How would this help people worship better?

3. Standing was once the customary posture throughout the Mass. That is why medieval cathedrals do not have pews. Can you imagine your own church without pews or chairs? How would that make the room feel? What would Mass feel like if folks were free to walk around? Does the seating in the church help or hinder people from standing, sitting and kneeling or from moving in procession?

4. In most parishes, people kneel from the "Holy, holy" until the Great Amen that concludes the eucharistic prayer. But in more and more parishes, in a return to tradition, people stand during this time. What difference does the choice of postures make at this point of the Mass? What attitudes do each reflect?

5. People who rarely go to church often will joke that they need guidance when to do what at Mass. Imagine that you need to explain to someone when (and perhaps why) we stand, sit or kneel. It might be helpful to make something of a chart of the parts of Mass and the posture during each part. What pattern do you notice in the chart?

6. What does the homily mean that our posture at worship — standing, sitting, kneeling — is a kind of rehearsal for how we live all week long?

HOMILY IX

MOVEMENT

People who study the doings of the tribes from which we all descend will tell us this: It is not easy to separate the two things we call worship and dance. For most of us, dancing is something that couples do at weddings, that people with strong ethnic traditions do on their holidays, that some very hard working folks do in modern dance and ballet companies. But in this room on Sundays? Worship and dance seem to have parted ways long ago in Western Christianity.

Not so, of course, in other parts of the world. If dance is an ordered movement of one or many bodies, often accompanied by music, then dance is very much a part of religious worship in Asia and Africa and the Middle East as it continues to be a part of the life and worship that belongs to Native Americans from both continents. Where we can witness this way of prayer — whether it be Zulu or Lakota or Hindu — we usually see that the movements we call dance are not reserved for leaders but belong to the whole community. Some people may have special parts to take, but everyone is caught up in the movement.

Why should dancing and worship be so linked for so many people? What is it about a community gathered to praise or to beseech God, to initiate newcomers or to bury their dead, that leads to music and to dance? One part of the answer has to do with this: A community praying is a community. It is not that several hundred people happen to find themselves in the same room at the same time, as they might at a department store, and each goes about his or her own tasks. When those who share one faith come together to give expression to that faith, then they act with some sort of unity — a unity that needs to be heard in song and a unity that needs to be seen in the posture and the movement of their bodies. That is the way human beings have found that things work. Here, we are many people doing a common task. To make that happen, there is an order here, a flow to things. We are all to be at home in this liturgy. It is not my show; it is our privilege, our duty. The movements of this liturgy are ordered movements. If they are not so, then they can't belong to all of us. And that is why worship and dance have such a long story together. Only dance, which is just ordered and practiced movement, can carry the day.

Now it may not look like dance any more, but maybe our notion of dance is not wide enough. Whatever we wish to call it, the movements in the liturgy are ordered movements. Yours are, mine are, the movements of lectors and communion ministers and servers are. And all our movements together are ordered. We don't need to call it a dance, this movement we do together on Sundays in this room, but we do need to know that the movements make a difference. Like the music, they build us up as a church or they tear us down. They are not neutral.

Look at just a few of the movements of our Sunday eucharist. The liturgy, like any assembly of people, has to begin and has to end with movement: gathering and going out. The gathering is like a great procession that begins in dozens and hundreds of places each Sunday, all around this community, and ends in one place, this room. One by one, three by three, five by five, the individuals and the households and the friends arrive here, converging from all over, bringing with us all those worlds where we live and work and worry. We pass through an entranceway, maybe not the grand porches and gathering areas of some churches, but however humble, there is our door, and on this side of it is this great hall, this room that takes its name from our name, "church."

Inside, the little processions perform some common actions. We take water on our hands, water that is meant to remind us of the baptism waters where we once put death to death and put on the life of Christ. With that water on our faces and bodies, we enter among other baptized people. We may greet some friends and some strangers alike as we find a place in this assembly. All of these small processions are then brought to their conclusion as the presider and other ministers walk through the midst of the assembly. Their procession is only the end of all these processions. They pass through the midst of the assembly here. That is not a way to get from the back of the room to the front of the room. This room has no back and has no front. The procession binds all who have gathered here into one assembly, a church ready to do its Sunday work. In their special clothing, with all of us singing our songs, the processing ministers are the tail end of this great movement, a climax that brings into our midst the book of God's word and then sets us down ready to hear that word and celebrate the eucharist.

In the liturgy of the word, the dance is in the way we sit to listen to the first two readings and then stand to face the reader of the gospel. And the dance is the Alleluia-accompanied procession that takes us to that gospel proclamation. Like all dance, this is wasted motion. It doesn't accomplish anything. It is totally inefficient. The gospel could be read from anywhere. It could be read without a parade from point A to point B. But this gathering is not about efficiency, it is about beauty and about spirit and about faith. And that is why our language here is poetry and dance, silence and song.

In a few moments we will begin the preparation of this table and its gifts. Again, there would be far more efficient ways than our procession carrying bread and wine to set the table. But we are concerned here with basic things that are also immense things: real bread and real wine, good gifts carried to the table by various people from our community. And when we have prayed over these gifts, giving God thanks and praise for all the work of creation and for the saving death and resurrection of Jesus, then we again process toward the table, this time to receive the body and the blood of our Lord Jesus Christ. After a short while, we take leave of one another and of this house, processing now into our Sunday, into our week, into all this world.

It isn't hard to see why the church went for most of its life without anything like pews. What's the use of seating to a people on the move, to a people engaged in this ritual dancing — all these processions and postures and other gestures — that we do together each Sunday? And that image, the dancing of this assembly, is perhaps the only way to break out of our deeply held notion that the Mass is something some people do for others, something that a few people do while others watch. If we want to compare the Mass to other sorts of human activity, we wouldn't choose a movie or a play or a baseball game. At these events, most of the people are spectators, on the sidelines.

For a real comparison to the Mass, we would have to choose a folk dance, a circle dance, something that was alive in nearly every culture until this century and is still a part of many societies. In such a dance, no one is a spectator, everyone is a participant. There may be leaders, but each person knows the steps and is at home in the dance. And the dance does its work. It makes the invisible community visible. It is an image of what life in this world is all about. It is the spirit of that life, and it somehow shows each dancer how to keep on when the dance seems to end.

Our Sunday liturgy is a circle dance with many movements we all know: taking the holy water and signing the body as we enter, bows and genuflections, signs of the cross great and small, greetings of peace, taking bread and cup in the hands, even reaching into pocket or purse for some financial sharing, some pooling of our resources to get our common work accomplished. All these things we know well to do. Let us give each movement, each gesture, a fullness that is new each Sunday.

The bulletin insert on the next two pages can be reproduced, added to the parish bulletin or handed out after Mass. The shorter version that follows it can be typed into the bulletin if space is limited.

MOVING HOME

All of our lives, it seems, we are learning to move in different ways. When we were infants, our parents looked for the movement of our eyes following their faces. They rejoiced at the moments when we could hold our heads up by ourselves, turn ourselves over, scoot across the floor on our stomachs, crawl on our hands and knees, raise ourselves to a standing position and, finally, walk unaided into their waiting arms. Soon we were running, skipping, bike riding, skateboarding, swimming and borrowing the family car. Games and sports taught us the importance of cooperating with others as we move toward a common goal. Parades showed us that getting there was at least half the fun; public transportation and traffic jams made us doubt it. After an illness or accident, we are anxious to get back on our feet, and if that's not possible, we are eager to learn to move on crutches or in wheelchairs. Movement is an essential part of our lives.

To most of us, dancing is something we may do at weddings or to celebrate our ethnic heritage. In many cultures, dance is a primary means of expression. In many parts of the world, everyone dances; i.e., moves together to worship, to grieve, to welcome, to celebrate.

It may seem odd to think of our liturgy as a movement. On the contrary, we have been well taught that liturgy is a place where we move as little as possible. But, in fact, our liturgy, our act of common worship, is a series of ordered movements—a dance, in many ways.

Dozens or hundreds of small processions, on foot, in cars or vans or busses, or on bicycle—in some places, even on horseback—bring us together to join our brothers and sisters in the worship that begins formally with song and movement. We stand and sing, sign ourselves with the cross, pause for silence and pray. We sit and raise our faces toward the one who proclaims God's word. We stand and participate in the gospel procession with our alleluias. We pray over our gifts of bread and wine and process again to receive the body and blood of our Lord Jesus Christ. Soon we process yet again, into our Sundays, back to our homes and work and world until the dance begins again when we next go to eucharist. It is a circle dance, one that ends to begin again, a dance made up of dozens of movements, small and large — bows and genuflections, signs of the cross, hands held out to receive bread and wine, gestures of peace. We learn these movements, as we learned to crawl and walk and ride a bike, not for the sake of learning them but to bring us somewhere — home to the reign of God.

Preaching about the Mass, © 1992 Archdiocese of Chicago, Liturgy Training Publications, 1800 North Hermitage Avenue, Chicago IL 60622-1101; 1-800-933-1800. Text by Victoria M. Tufano. Design by Jill Smith.

MOVING HOME

Our liturgy is a dance in many ways. Dozens of small processions bring us together. We stand and sing, pause for silence, and pray. We sit and raise our faces toward the one who proclaims God's word. We stand and sing our alleluias, pray over our gifts of bread and wine, and process to receive the body and blood of our Lord Jesus Christ. Soon, we process again, back to our homes and work and world. It is a dance made up of dozens of movements — bows and genuflections, signs of the cross, hands held out to receive bread and wine, gestures of peace. We learn these movements, as we learned to crawl and walk and ride a bike, not simply for the sake of learning them, but to bring us somewhere — home to the reign of God.

Preaching about the Mass, © 1992 Archdiocese of Chicago, Liturgy Training Publications, 1800 North Hermitage Avenue, Chicago IL 60622-1101; 1-800-933-1800. Text by Victoria M. Tufano. Design by Jill Smith.

REFLECTION QUESTIONS

1. Spoken instead of sung prayer would feel weird to many people in the world. The same thing can be said about prayer without dance; it would seem odd, maybe even irreverent. Why do you think we sometimes feel almost the opposite? What in our culture makes us uncomfortable with ritual movement?

2. Imagine the Mass in your parish church done in mime — in complete silence, with no "props." What motions does everyone go through? Are these movements done deliberately, broadly and elegantly, or are they done hastily and haphazardly?

3. Has anyone ever taught the congregation the appropriate way to make the sign of the cross, to sign oneself at the gospel, to give the sign of peace, to come forward to receive communion, even how to sit and stand in a graceful manner? Gestures aren't necessarily picked up by observation; perhaps they need to be demonstrated and explained with care. How are they taught to new Catholics or to the children of the parish?

4. Many people say they enjoy processions or at least that they have fond memories of being in processions. What are your memories of religious processions? Imagine that you are responsible for organizing one. What would you need to be concerned about? Is the communion procession at Mass well organized — is it graceful or clumsy, joyful or dour?

5. Have you ever participated in folk dancing where everyone joins in? (Square dancing is like that.) It may seem odd reasoning to compare dancing to Mass, but how is a square dance like liturgy?

6. The Roman rite looks like a communal dance when done well. And to be done well, it needs a floor plan that is arranged for it to happen. This is something that perhaps has to be experienced to be believed. Does the floor plan in your church allow for the easy movement of the assembly?

HOMILY X

Some years ago the comedian George Carlin had a routine about the word "stuff." He pointed out how we always have to go and get our "stuff." "I'll be right with you, as soon as I get my stuff." "Hey, where'd you put my stuff?" "I don't know. Is this your stuff in the corner?"

Right? When we get ready to go to work in the morning, don't we first make sure we've got our stuff? Or we put all our stuff in the car and go off on a long weekend. It seems we human beings seldom are empty-handed.

Certainly not when we come here together on Sunday. We Catholics bring our stuff along. In fact, should we come empty-handed we would have to do something other than the eucharist together because the eucharist needs human stuff. It isn't some abstraction, some pleasant act of imagination. It is the Catholic people bringing some stuff with them for their assembly.

First there is the stuff we have but could do without in a pinch. The furniture, for example. We have these benches and chairs and pews where we sit. The church did without those for most of its history, and in fact they often keep us from being an active assembly. There is also this place here, this piece of furniture called the pulpit or lectern or ambo, from which the word is read and the homily preached. It is useful and should be built to give good service and show respect for the word of God that is proclaimed here. But we could get by without it.

The two pieces of furniture we would have the hardest time doing without are the font and the table. The font holds the water, the table the bread and wine. They have important work to do, and in our tradition, each — the font and the table — has itself come to be an image of God's presence. They should be so worthily made and maintained that they bear the weight of their task. The font must present itself as the womb from which Christians are born, the tomb in which the old self is buried. And the altar is called by Christ's name, is kissed in reverence as the liturgy begins and ends, for it serves to center our community in the praise of God as we make the eucharistic prayer and partake of the holy communion.

But in a pinch, we could do without the font. Christians have always baptized in streams and rivers and bathhouses and wherever water was available in large quantities. And we could do without the table. Christians have used the table of the earth itself, the floors of prisons, and tiny tables in hospitals. When we have a place where a stable congregation assembles each Sunday, then we want to give attention to the font and the table. What stuff is essential here? What do we have to have? Probably only three things. We need our book, our bread and our wine.

First, our book. The book that is called the lectionary (meaning a book of readings) is brought into this room at the beginning of the liturgy, held high. It contains the readings from scripture arranged in order for the seasons and Sundays of the year. Already at the time of Jesus, it was the practice for Jewish people to gather and read from their scriptures. That reading would be the beginning point for commentary and discussion. The followers of Jesus continued to carry with them the holy scriptures, gradually adding the gospels and the letters that we call the New Testament. In the assemblies of Christians the book would be opened and the scriptures read aloud. And that has been our tradition always.

The church — this church right here today — goes nowhere without the scriptures. The church never passes a Sunday without gathering and opening the book for public reading. The words that we read are arranged in an order. We don't decide that we would like to hear this or that reading today. We follow the order of the lectionary, reading slowly through the gospels, the letters, and some — but too few — parts of the Hebrew Scriptures, the Old Testament. We don't make up our faith new every Sunday. Rather, we carry this book to the church every Sunday. We hold this book high in our processions, and it is honored with incense on special days, and it is kissed each Sunday after the gospel. It is just this humble thing — just some ink on some paper, bound up and sewn together — but for us it is our access to the word of God: "To whom shall we go? You have the words of everlasting life."

Bread and wine are the other necessities. Sometimes, when the church has been powerful and rich, it has seemed to be almost embarrassed about these two ordinary substances. Then, we brought out vessels of silver and gold, sparkling with jewels even. And we treated the bread and wine as if we wished they would disappear altogether. The bread lost the look of bread, the smell of bread, the texture of bread and the taste of bread. And the wine would ordinarily be one swallow for one person, and that swallow would be hidden in the bottom of a large and heavy chalice.

In the last generation that began to change — slowly. This simple bread, made without any ingredients except flour and water, this bread of the very poor, now sometimes does look like bread and taste like bread. And the wine, the drink that brings delight and lifted spirits to our tables, is there at more and more liturgies to be seen, smelled, taken by all in the holy communion.

Bread and wine challenge most of us. We are used to fast foods and foods made from many ingredients and sometimes exotic foods. But here are the foods of a common table, the same for rich and poor, old and young, women and men:

one and all invited and commanded — take and eat — to have a piece broken from the one loaf of bread, one and all invited — take and drink — to put the common cup to our lips and taste and see.

Isn't it strange — almost funny, almost a scandal — that in the center of our Sunday assembly, at the very heart of what we do together week after week to manifest and to make strong our faith, at the center of this is a table with nothing costly, nothing rare, nothing of any real note at all on it, but just enough bread for all to taste, just enough wine for all to have a sip?

How then do we handle this bread and this wine? They are brought forward with simple reverence because they are the "fruit of the earth and the work of human hands." They are both: fruit of the earth is God's doing, but work of human hands is ours. In worthy vessels — a plate, a large cup — they rest on the table around which we stand to give God praise and thanks in the memory of Jesus' death and resurrection. We pray that "they may become for us the body and blood of our Lord, Jesus Christ." Then we process to the table with song and answer Amen to the proclamation: "The body of Christ." "The blood of Christ."

Everything else is secondary to the book, the bread and the wine. But secondary is not unimportant. When we have candles, when we have the cross, when we have incense or banners, when we have a certain vesture for those with responsibilities to the assembly, when we have vessels for the water that is used to sprinkle us during Eastertime and vessels for our money when it is collected — all of these and anything else we use are to express the grace and the beauty and very often the simplicity that we meet in our book, our bread and our wine. How we handle these objects here is not to be measured by some sacredness that comes with their being used in the liturgy. Rather, how we handle them is to

reflect and to build up how we handle all the work of creation and all the work of human hands. Fifteen centuries
ago, St. Benedict told his followers to treat the vessels of the
kitchen as they would the vessels of the altar. That is
exactly the point. Here we learn how to live day by day with
the wonder and beauty of God's work and our own.

The bulletin insert on the next two pages can be reproduced, added to
the parish bulletin or handed out after Mass. The shorter version that
follows it can be typed into the bulletin if space is limited.

HOMILY X

97

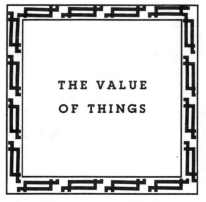

THE VALUE OF THINGS

Never underestimate the value of things. Look around you the next time you are in church. Look at the various objects, the things. What, in your opinion, could go? What are the important things? What are the things you would change if you could?

The pews? (That's the pew where Joanie sat when she made her first communion! And there's the pew where Paul finally was able to break down and cry after his brother was killed. Remember Ann Simpson? — she sat in that pew every day at Mass — I really miss her.)

The baptismal font? (Look at that! Mary's daughter, grandson, and her twin great-grandsons — all baptized in that very same font.)

The stained-glass windows? (Joe's family saved for two years to get his mother's name engraved on a nameplate on that window.)

The processional cross, the ambo, the vestments? All were probably donated in someone's memory.

It's true, these are only things, and not even the essential things for liturgy. But the fact is that they are valuable, not because they cost a lot of money but because of what people have invested in them. They are sacred even, because peoples' lives, stories and memories are contained in them.

So let us be sensitive when we use the objects in our church; let us be honest but gentle when the objects need to be replaced or removed; and let us be patient with those who don't understand and who find such changes difficult.

And let us pay particular attention to the simple essentials. Is this lectionary our most beautiful book? Is ours the most delicious bread we can bring? Is our wine the best we can offer? Let us not forget that this book *is* the word of

God, Jesus Christ, and that this bread and this wine *is* his body and his blood — and so these simple, beautiful things are the only ones we truly need for liturgy.

Preaching about the Mass, © 1992 Archdiocese of Chicago, Liturgy Training Publications, 1800 North Hermitage Avenue, Chicago IL 60622-1101; 1-800-933-1800. Text by Theresa Pincich. Design by Jill Smith.

THE VALUE OF THINGS

Never underestimate the value of things. Look around you the next time you are in church. Look at the objects, the things. What, in your opinion, could go? What are the important things? What are the things you would change if you could?

The pews? The baptismal font? The processional cross, the ambo, the vestments?

These are only things, not even the essential things for liturgy. But they are sacred because of what people have invested in them—their lives and stories and memories.

So let us use the objects in our churches with reverence. Let us pay attention to the simple essentials, so that the lectionary is our most beautiful book, our bread the most delicious we can bring, and our wine the best we can find. For in these simple things, Christ comes to us.

Preaching about the Mass, © 1992 Archdiocese of Chicago, Liturgy Training Publications, 1800 North Hermitage Avenue, Chicago IL 60622-1101; 1-800-933-1800. Text by Theresa Pincich. Design by Jill Smith.

REFLECTION QUESTIONS

1. The homily suggests a telling exercise: Make a list of the objects used in worship—everything from flowers to microphones. Which are essential on Sundays? Which are important, and while not essential, make for better liturgy? Are the objects well crafted and well maintained? Can you see the "work of human hands" in them?

2. In ancient times at worship there was a tradition of bringing in objects only when they were to be used and then removing them after use. If the object was too big to carry (like a font), then the *people* moved to it during its use. Can you imagine the layout of a church where people move from lectern to font to altar, with enough room for all this to happen gracefully? During the liturgy in your own church, do any objects distract you from focusing on what is happening?

3. The old-fashioned word "sacristan" is used for the ministry of the caretakers of the belongings of the church. Many parishes are realizing that this ministry is, more than ever, a necessary and time-consuming job. Who are your church's sacristans? How well are they trained for this demanding task? Are they compensated for their time? Do they have a worthy budget with which to work?

4. What holy things do you have in the house? What objects do you use to celebrate special times? What sort of memories are attached to the "stuff" in your home? Do you consider the supper table holy? How about the bathtub?

RESOURCES

The following resources are useful for looking at the way liturgy is done in your parish:

Bernardin, Joseph Cardinal. *Our Communion, Our Peace, Our Promise: Pastoral Letter on the Liturgy.* Chicago: Liturgy Training Publications, 1984.

> Written *to* the assembly, this letter is a straightforward discussion of the Mass. Also available, *Study Guide for Group Discussion about the Mass* helps readers use the letter to evaluate parish practice. Available in Spanish, English, Polish and Italian.

Hoffman, Elizabeth, ed. *The Liturgy Documents.* Chicago: Liturgy Training Publications, 1991.

> The major documents, including *Fulfilled in Your Hearing* (quoted earlier) are compiled with helpful and brief introductions.

Huck, Gabe. *Liturgy with Style and Grace.* Chicago: Liturgy Training Publications, 1984.

> Short chapters, each with reflection questions that guide groups or individuals in a thorough examination of what liturgy is and how it can best be enacted. This book is excellent for the parish staff or liturgy committee to use over the course of a year or two.

Keifer, Ralph. *To Hear and Proclaim.* Washington DC: The Pastoral Press, 1983.

> The *Introduction to the Lectionary* is reprinted in this book with a good and practical commentary on how to enact it.

Keifer, Ralph. *To Give Thanks and Praise.* Washington DC: The Pastoral Press, 1986.

> The *General Instruction of the Roman Missal* is reprinted in this book with a good and practical commentary on how to use it in preparing liturgy. The suggestions about the entrance rites are particularly good.

These books are good for further study:

Cabié, Robert. *The Eucharist.* Collegeville MN: The Liturgical Press, 1986.

> A short, scholarly study of the historical development of the Mass.

Foley, Edward. *From Age to Age.* Chicago: Liturgy Training Publications, 1991.

> A scholarly narrative of the history and meaning of the Mass as seen through the development of architecture, music, books and vessels.

Mauck, Marchita. *Shaping a House for the Church.* Chicago: Liturgy Training Publications, 1990.

> A major but subtle reason why our celebrations of the liturgy fail is because of the physical environment in which we gather. Renewed rites need renewed places of worship. Read this book to begin analyzing the appropriateness of your own church building.

Parker, Alice. *Melodious Accord: Good Singing in Church.* Chicago: Liturgy Training Publications, 1991.

> The importance of song in liturgy cannot be overstated. This book argues that our assemblies *can* sing well and offers some suggestions as to how.

For more materials to include in the parish bulletin:

Ciferni, Andrew. *Environment for Catholic Worship.* Washington DC: Federation of Diocesan Liturgical Commissions, 1988.

> This is a packet of 11 handouts explaining the function of the church interior and sacred images. Each handout is a two-sided, 8½-by-11-inch sheet laid out to be folded. Line drawings are included throughout. The price is determined by how many copies you will make.

Give Thanks and Praise. Washington DC: Federation of Diocesan Liturgical Commissions, 1987.

> This packet of ten handouts explains the Mass in a two-sided, 8½-by-11-inch format. The price is determined by how many copies you will make.

Addresses and phone numbers of publishers:

Federation of Diocesan Liturgical Commissions
PO Box 29039
Washington DC 20017
202-635-6990

The Liturgical Press
St. John's Abbey
PO Box 7500
Collegeville MN 56321-7500
320-363-2213

Liturgy Training Publications
1800 North Hermitage Avenue
Chicago IL 60622-1101
1-800-933-1800

Pastoral Press
225 Sheridan Street NW
Washington DC 20011-1492
202-723-5800